TABLE OF CONTENTS

The Coast Guard Intelligence Program Enters the Intelligence Community

A Case Study of Congressional Influence on Intelligence Community Evolution

Occasional Paper Number Sixteen

Kevin E. Wirth
LCDR, U.S. Coast Guard

NDIC PRESS

National Defense Intelligence College
Washington, DC
May 2007

The National Defense Intelligence College supports and encourages research that distills lessons and improves Intelligence Community capabilities for policy-level and operational consumers

The Coast Guard Intelligence Program Enters the Intelligence Community: A Case Study of Congressional Influence on Intelligence Community Evolution, Kevin E. Wirth

This series of Occasional Papers presents the work of faculty, students, and others whose research on intelligence issues is supported or otherwise encouraged by the National Defense Intelligence College. Occasional Papers are distributed to Department of Defense schools and to the Intelligence Community, and unclassified papers are available to the public through the National Technical Information Service (*www.ntis. gov*). Selected papers are also available through the U.S. Government Printing Office (*www.gpo.gov*).

This work builds on earlier publications in this series, particularly Occasional Paper Number Nine, The Creation of the National Imagery and Mapping Agency: Congress's Role as Overseer, by Anne Daugherty Miles. The author of the present paper has examined how the Coast Guard became a member of the Intelligence Community, how Congress was involved, and how Congress will likely be increasingly involved in the organization of the Community. Derived from a thesis completed in 2003, this paper illustrates the importance of gathering electronic data immediately, since much of the reference material on which this study is based existed only as informal e-mail or documents stored on computers. Much of it likely would have been erased had the research started even a year later.

Proposed manuscripts for these papers are submitted for consideration to the NDIC Press Editorial Board. Papers undergo review by senior officials in Defense, Intelligence, and civilian academic or business communities. Manuscripts or requests for additional copies of Occasional Papers should be addressed to Defense Intelligence Agency, National Defense Intelligence College, MC-X, Bolling AFB, Washington, DC 20340-5100.

This publication has been approved for unrestricted distribution by the Office of Security Review, Department of Defense.

James E. Lightfoot, Editor and Associate Director
Center for Strategic Intelligence Research
James.lightfoot@dia.mil

LIST OF FIGURES

FOREWORD

Although the United States Coast Guard has utilized intelligence capabilities since the service's inception in 1790, the Coast Guard was not included as a formal member of the Intelligence Community until December 2002. From the days of Revenue Cutter Captains walking the docks, to its pioneering use of signals intelligence during prohibition, and with today's use of national technical means, many Coast Guard successes rely on intelligence. As a regulatory entity, a law enforcement agency, a military service, and as the premier domestic maritime agency, every day the Coast Guard executes a very broad area of mission responsibility.

Prior to 2002, the Coast Guard contributed to and benefited from Intelligence Community analysis as a customer. However, increasing transnational threats such as drug smuggling, weapons proliferation, and illegal migration, some involving or supporting terrorist organizations, accentuated the need for and the benefit of Coast Guard membership within the Intelligence Community.

Mr. Wirth describes the story behind the short but significant amendment to the National Security Act of 1947 which resulted in the Coast Guard's formal entry into the Intelligence Community. Researched within eighteen months of passage, this case study exhaustively documents extensive congressional and Coast Guard staff work. Interviews at the action officer level clearly reveal the view from the bureaucratic trenches, and additional attention to talking points, meeting minutes, and email summaries add immediacy as they further clarify positions from within departments, staffs and agencies. A brief examination of the surrounding political and geopolitical events, such as the bombing of the USS *Cole*, political changes in Congress, internal Coast Guard actions, and the tragic attacks of September 11th, provide context to the passage of this provision.

As a member of the Intelligence Community, the Coast Guard has succeeded in combining law enforcement and intelligence contributions not only to be always ready to respond to all threats and all hazards, but as a model for the post-September 11th world of intelligence.

James F. Sloan
Assistant Commandant for Intelligence and Criminal Investigations
United States Coast Guard

SELECTED ACRONYMS

AEC – Atomic Energy Commission
AOR – Area of Responsibility
BAH – Booz Allen & Hamilton
CCP – Consolidated Cryptologic Program
CGIP – Coast Guard Intelligence Program
CIA – Central Intelligence Agency
CIO – Central Imagery Office
CMS – Community Management Staff
CNI – Center for Naval Intelligence
CT – Counterterrorism
D14 – Coast Guard District 14
DCI – Director of Central Intelligence
DCP – Defense Cryptologic Program
DDCI (CM) – Deputy Director of Central Intelligence for
Community Management
DEA – Drug Enforcement Agency
DGIAP – Defense General Intelligence Applications Program
DHS – Department of Homeland Security
DIA – Defense Intelligence Agency
DIMAP – Defense Imagery and Mapping Program
DIRNSA – Director, National Security Agency
DOD – Department of Defense
DOJ – Department of Justice
DOT – Department of Transportation
EO - Executive Order
FBI – Federal Bureau of Investigation
FY – Fiscal Year
G-C – Commandant of the Coast Guard
G-O – Assistant Commandant for Operations
GDIP – General Defense Intelligence Program
HAC – House Appropriations Committee
HAC-D – House Appropriations Committee, subcommittee on defense
HASC – House Armed Services Committee
HPSCI – House Permanent Select Committee on Intelligence
HUMINT – Human Intelligence
I2STC - Intelligence and Investigations Standardization and Development Center
IA/IP – Information Analysis and Infrastructure Protection division of DHS
IAC – Intelligence Advisory Committee
IC – Intelligence Community
IC21 – Intelligence Community in the 21st Century
ICC – Intelligence Coordination Center
IDS – Integrated Deepwater System
IG – Inspector General
INR – State Department Bureau of Intelligence and Research

I-POM – Intelligence Program Objective Memorandum
IS – Intelligence Specialist (not yet a rating in USCG; yes in USN)
JCS – Joint Chiefs of Staff
JIATF – Joint Interagency Task Force
JMIP – Joint Military Intelligence Program
MOA – Memorandum of Agreement
MTS – Marine Transport System
NGA – National Geospatial-Intelligence Agency
NGP – National Geospatial-Intelligence Program
NIMA – National Imagery and Mapping Agency (predecessor to NGA)
NRO – National Reconnaissance Organization
NRP – National Reconnaissance Program
NSA – National Security Agency
NSC – National Security Council
OCI – Office of Counterintelligence
OMB – Office of Management and Budget
ONI – Office of Naval Intelligence
ONS – Office of National Security
OSS – Office of Strategic Services
P.L. – Public Law
PACOM – U.S. Pacific Command
S-1 – Secretary of Transportation (S-2 Deputy Secretary, etc)
SAC – Senate Appropriations Committee
SAP – Statement of Administrative Policy
SASC – Senate Armed Services Committee
SECDEF – Secretary of Defense
SECDOT – Secretary of Transportation
SOUTHCOM – U.S. Southern Command
SSCI – Senate Select Committee on Intelligence
SSG – Senior Steering Group
TIARA – Tactical Intelligence and Related Activities
USAF – United States Air Force
USC – United States Code
USCG – United States Coast Guard
USCIB – United States Communications Board
USIB – United States Intelligence Board
USMC – United States Marine Corps
USN – United States Navy
WMD – Weapons of Mass Destruction

A SEAT AT THE TABLE

Sec. 105. Codification of the Coast Guard as an Element of the Intelligence Community.

Section 3(4)(H) of the National Security Act of 1947 (50 U.S.C. 401a(4)(H)) is amended—
    (1) by striking 'and' before 'the Department of Energy'; and
    (2) by inserting ', and the Coast Guard' before the semicolon.

– Intelligence Authorization Act for Fiscal Year 2002

With this amendment to the *National Security Act of 1947,* the *Intelligence Authorization Act for Fiscal Year 2002* mandated the inclusion of Coast Guard's National Intelligence Element formally into the National Foreign Intelligence Community (IC). For decades the Coast Guard had collected foreign intelligence through its accredited attachés, through exploitation of ship visits and through other media. The Coast Guard's broad mission responsibilities and record of joint operations with Defense Department agencies catalyzed its placement in the IC. This amendment was the culmination of more than three years of studies and meetings aimed at getting the Coast Guard a "seat at the table." Although the words in the legislation were few, the ramifications of Coast Guard membership in the Community are potentially great.

Despite a long relationship with the Intelligence Community, the Coast Guard's formal membership in the IC emerged as a result of the changing international threat environment, an increased need for Coast Guard access, and the advocacy of the House Permanent Select Committee on Intelligence (HPSCI). Using primary archival sources, this manuscript describes how the bureaucratic ossification of the Intelligence Community, and the changing political and national security environment, resulted in unprecedented Congressional action adding the Coast Guard Intelligence Program to the Intelligence Community despite the opposition of the Director of Central Intelligence. Traditional IC tendencies to protect resources and to maintain the status quo prompted Congress to effect dramatic institutional change. This case study examines congressional relationships with the IC. The process of Coast Guard entry into the Intelligence Community fits a trend, that of an increasingly formalized Intelligence Community as a concomitant of more active congressional oversight. This case illustrates how the "Intelligence Community" continues to evolve from an abstract concept toward a more clearly defined federation of government offices and agencies. In brief, it tracks the "operationalization" of the "Intelligence Community" as a concept. [1]

The Research Question

Coast Guard Intelligence "specialties" include countering illegal smuggling of weapons, drugs, and migrants. Countering these continuing threats to U.S. National Security requires timely and accurate intelligence information on states and on elusive non-state actors. The President's National Security Strategy calls for the Intelligence Community to "transform our intelligence capabilities and build new ones to keep pace with" threats generated by a "complex and elusive set of targets." [2] In addition to collection against new targets, the possibility of domestic terrorist attacks demands "the proper fusion of information between intelligence and law enforcement." [3] This call for transformation to collect against new targets and fuse information requires organizational changes to the U.S. Intelligence Community. Coast Guard entry into the Community is an early but dramatic change. Who initiates such organizational change and how it is carried out interest Community members, since those changes could be made in unprecedented ways. Will Congress continue to take the lead in IC reformation and change for the coming years?

Specifically the research question addressed here is "How may Coast Guard's inclusion into the Intelligence Community through a HPSCI-sponsored initiative affect the future modification and management of the Intelligence Community?" The key questions that guide the exploration are:

Why did Congress initiate this change to the IC membership?

How has the IC evolved and what role has Congress played historically?

What impact did external events have on the decision to include the Coast Guard Intelligence Program?

---

1 "Operationalization" refers to the process of making concepts increasingly specific and more subject to description, categorization and measurement: "the concrete and specific definition of something in terms of the operations by which observations are to be categorized." Earl Babbie, *The Practice of Social Research*, 6th ed. (Belmont, CA: Wadsworth Publishing, 1992), 80, G6. Another way of describing "operationalization" is "putting theory into practice."

2 U. S. President, "The National Security Strategy of the United States of America," 27 September 2002, 30. Cited hereafter as National Security Strategy.

3 National Security Strategy, 30.

Definitions and Scope

What is the "Intelligence Community?" The original *National Security Act of 1947* neither listed nor defined the members of the Intelligence Community.[4] General Mark Clark first used the term in a 1955 report to Congress.[5] The IC defines itself as "a federation of executive branch agencies and organizations that work separately and together to conduct intelligence activities necessary for the conduct of foreign relations and the protection of the national security of the United States."[6] Many organizations and agencies qualify for designation as IC members under this definition. Membership would depend on the individual interpretation of "conduct of intelligence activities." A specific list of the members of the Intelligence Community was added to section 401 (a) of the *National Security Act of 1947* by the *Intelligence Authorization Act for Fiscal Year 1993.*[7]

Congressional and executive agency actions occur in a contested action-space that exists between veto by the President and funding or legislative restrictions enacted by the Congress. There is a tacit recognition that should either Congress or the executive branch disapprove strongly enough, either branch of government has the capability to prevent or constrain the actions of the other.

The Coast Guard has used and developed intelligence capabilities since the service's inception in 1789. As an armed service and law enforcement agency, its counter-smuggling missions involved collection and generation of operational intelligence.[8] During the 1980s the counterdrug smuggling mission emphasized increased intelligence requirements and spurred partnerships between the IC and the Coast Guard. The present-day Joint Interagency Task Forces East and West, which are "Joint Operations Command Center[s] where intelligence and operations functions are fused,"[9] exist to meet the increased need for counter-smuggling intelligence. Although the intelligence capabilities of the Coast Guard

---

4 U.S. Congress, House, Permanent Select Committee on Intelligence, *Compilation of Intelligence Laws and Related Laws and Executive Orders of Interest to the National Intelligence Community,* 99th Congress, 1st session, 1985, Committee Print, 4.

5 The term "Intelligence Community" is attributed to: Commission on Organization of the Executive Branch of the Government, A Report to the Congress, *Intelligence Activities,* June 1955. Cited in Richard A. Best Jr., and Herbert Boerstling, "Proposals for Intelligence Reorganization, 1949-1996," (A report prepared for the Permanent Select Committee on Intelligence, House of Representatives) *Congressional Research Service* (Washington, DC: Congressional Research Service, Library of Congress, 28 February 1996), 13. This report is attached as appendix C to U.S. Congress, House, Permanent Select Committee on Intelligence Staff Study, *IC21: Intelligence Community in the 21st Century,* 104th Congress (Washington, DC: GPO, 1996).

6 *Intelligence Community Homepage,* "Definition of the Intelligence Community," URL: <http: http://www.intelligence.gov/1-definition.shtml>, accessed 11 July 2003.

7 Title VII, section 3 of Public Law 102-496, *Intelligence Authorization Act for Fiscal Year 1993.*

8 One review of the Coast Guard's path-breaking intelligence efforts is Eric S. Ensign, Lieutenant Commander USCG, *Intelligence in the Rum War at Sea, 1920-1933* MSSI thesis (Washington: Joint Military Intelligence College, 2001).

9 "Fact Sheet", *Joint Interagency Task Force East Homepage.* URL:<http://www.jiatfe. southcom. mil/?cgFact>, accessed 8 May 2003. Cited hereafter as *JIATF east homepage.*

---

have long existed, the present work addresses only the actions of the Coast Guard Intelligence Staff directly involved in the IC membership initiative.[10]

Plan of the Study

The next section examines congressional oversight of the IC, the origins of IC members and evolution of the Community. After that, emphasis is on the use of legislation to shape the Community, and to modify the relationships between the IC and Congress. These considerations lead to a working hypothesis that Congress itself will lead IC reformation and change for the coming years.

In relating the "inside story" of Coast Guard entry into the National Foreign Intelligence Program, this study documents interagency and inter-branch rivalries and captures how Congress shaped the decision for IC membership. This study represents the first detailed written account of how the Coast Guard Intelligence Program entered the IC.

---

10 Some discussions of Coast Guard Intelligence history and operations include, Ensign, *Intelligence in the Rum War at Sea, 1920-1933*, Alex Larzelere, *Castro's Ploy—America's Dilemma: The 1980 Cuban Boatlift* (Washington: National Defense University Press, 1988); Charles M. Fuss, Jr., *Sea of Grass: The Maritime Drug War, 1970-1990* (Annapolis: Naval Institute Press, 1996); Ronald O'Rouke "Homeland Security: Coast Guard Operations-Background and Issues for Congress." *CRS Report for Congress* RS 21125 (Washington, DC: Congressional Research Service, Library of Congress, updated 8 October 2002); *The United States Coast Guard: America's Lifesaver and Guardian of the Seas: A Guide to the U.S. Coast Guard* (Tampa, FL: Faircourt LLC, 2002), available at URL: < http:// www.faircount.com/ web04/coast/index.html>, accessed 11 July 2003.

CONGRESSIONAL OVERSIGHT AND EVOLUTION OF COMMUNITY MEMBERSHIP

The U.S. Constitution establishes a system of checks and balances empowering the three branches of government with limited and intersecting powers. Congress can cut off funding for an initiative and pass laws specifically prohibiting executive branch actions. The President can veto any bill passed by the Congress. Despite the availability of these options, vetoes and funding restrictions can require the expenditure of political capital and consequently are infrequently used.[11]

In the U.S. system of government both branches must agree for any action to be viable, so they must achieve a consensus on an issue to make law. Should either branch object forcefully, steps are often taken to prevent passage or kill the initiative. For example, if the President or Congress objects to the addition of agencies into the IC, the member agency would be vetoed at creation or unfunded after creation. This section provides historical context for understanding the role of congressional oversight in the expansion and shaping of the Intelligence Community.

Article One, Section Eight of the Constitution establishes the broad powers of Congress. Clause One provides Congress the "power of the purse," placing final fiscal approval with Congress. Clause Nine gives Congress the power "to constitute Tribunals inferior to the Supreme Court"[12] and provides the basis for investigative hearings. The "elastic clause," Clause Eighteen, provides Congress the ability "to make all laws which shall be necessary and proper for carrying into Execution the forgoing Powers"[13] and provides one of the broadest foundations for oversight.

These and other constitutional powers have evolved over 225 years to form the principal tools of congressional oversight. The *Legislative Reorganization Act of 1946* placed primary oversight responsibility within the standing committees of the House of Representatives and the Senate, requiring them to exercise "continuous watchfulness." The passage of Senate Resolution 400 on 19 May 1976 created the Senate Select Committee on Intelligence (SSCI), the principal intelligence

---

11 President Clinton used 36 vetoes, President Reagan 78; both had eight years in office. Gary Galemore, "The Presidential Veto and Congressional Procedure," *CRS Report for Congress* 98-156 (Washington, DC: Congressional Research Service. Library of Congress, 29 January 2001), 3.

12 *U.S. Constitution,* art I, sec. 8.

13 *U.S. Constitution,* art I, sec. 8.

oversight committee for the Senate.[14] The House Permanent Select Committee on Intelligence (HPSCI) was formed one year later by passage of House Resolution 658.[15]

Intelligence Committees

Select Nature of Intelligence Committees

The HPSCI and SSCI are select committees that are permanent and can draft legislation. Members of select committees are chosen by the majority and minority leadership in each chamber. These committees have a narrow focus and overlapping jurisdiction with other committees. Their permanence and ability to legislate make them different from the other select committees which are usually temporary and investigative in nature. There are several tools of congressional oversight. With respect to the IC, the most commonly used include the power to write laws, hold hearings, authorize and appropriate funding, require reorganization, and demand that specific information be divulged.

Writing Law

Writing law is one of the most significant tools of congressional oversight. The Intelligence Oversight Act of 1980, the Boland amendments, and the amendments to the National Security Act of 1947[16] are examples of this oversight ability as exercised by the intelligence committees.

Hearings

A committee can call hearings to seek additional information on incidents, failures, or noteworthy issues. Sometimes hearings are stimulated by the news coverage in reaction to tragic events or scandals. The Iran-Contra hearings and the Church and Pike committee hearings are examples of special investigatory hearings. More common, but just as important, are Senate confirmation hearings. Confirmation is an arduous and easily politicized process. Many nominees withdraw based on pressure and fears.

When Robert Gates was nominated as Director of Central Intelligence (DCI) in 1987 (the first of two nominations to that position) he withdrew in the

---

14 Frank J. Smist Jr., *Congress Oversees the United States Intelligence Community 1947-1994*, 2nd ed. (Knoxville,TN: The University of Tennessee Press, 1994), 82-83. In a compromise, the Senate Armed Services Committee maintained oversight responsibility and budget authority for tactical intelligence.

15 Smist, 214-217.

16 The *Intelligence Oversight Act of 1980* required the executive branch to keep the HPSCI and SSCI "fully and currently informed" of all intelligence activities. The Boland Amendments prohibited the executive branch from providing funds to groups advocating the overthrow of the Nicaraguan and Honduran Government. The *National Security Act of 1947* created the DCI and CIA. Smist, 122, 248, and 3-5.

middle of a politically messy confirmation process.[17] During the second day of confirmation hearings in 1987, in response to a photographer's question about how he liked being DCI so far, Gates quipped "You know that country and western song, 'take this job and shove it'?" Despite some embarrassment over the subsequent broadcast of those remarks, Gates admitted "it accurately conveyed my sentiments."[18] During his second confirmation hearing he faced a maelstrom of questions and allegations, including "cooking the analysis" of the Russian threat to support Reagan administration policy.[19]

Congress has increased the number of positions requiring confirmation: "the Intelligence Authorization Act of 1997 established three new assistant directors of the Central Intelligence Agency (CIA) and a new deputy director for community management DDCI (CM), along with a statutory general counsel, all subject to Senate confirmation."[20] A Community Management Staff (CMS) of up to 303 people assists the DDCI (CM).[21] This staff represented the IC during the CGIP-IC entry process. Created in 1992, five years before this reorganization, by Director of Central Intelligence Directive 3/3, CMS functions include:

Developing, coordinating, and implementing DCI policy and exercising DCI responsibilities for the Intelligence Community in the following areas:

a. intelligence policy and planning;

b. National Foreign Intelligence Program and budget development, evaluation, justification, and monitoring;

c. intelligence requirements management and evaluation; and

d. performance of such other functions and duties as determined by the DCI, federal statutes, or executive action.

As part of these responsibilities, the Staff will identify cross-program trade-offs, establish divisions of labor, reduce unnecessary duplication of effort, evaluate competitive investment proposals, and identify efficiencies and cost savings throughout the Intelligence Community.[22]

---

17 Robert Gates, *From the Shadows. The Ultimate Insider's Story of Five Presidents and How they Won the Cold War* (New York: Simon and Schuster, 1996), 417-418.

18 Gates, 417.

19 Marvin C. Ott, "Partisanship and the Decline of Intelligence Oversight," *International Journal of Intelligence and Counterintelligence* 16, no. 1 (Spring 2003): 81-82; Gates, 542-552.

20 Stephen F. Knott, "The Great Republican Transformation on Oversight," *International Journal of Intelligence and Counterintelligence* 13, no. 1 (Spring 2000): 54.

21 Jeffery, T. Richelson, *The U.S. Intelligence Community* (Boulder, CO: Westview Press, 1999), 388-389.

22 Director of Central Intelligence, Director of Central Intelligence Directive 3/3, "Community Management Staff," 12 June 1995. *Federation of American Scientists Homepage,* URL: < http://www.fas.org/irp/offdocs/dcid3-3.htm>, accessed 5 July 2003; Richelson, 388.

The resource management office is one of three offices within CMS and is responsible for "National Foreign Intelligence Program (NFIP) budget development, evaluation, justification, and monitoring."[23] Their opposition to CGIP entry into the IC is portrayed later in this study.

The Power of the Purse

The "power of the purse," or authorization and appropriation, allows Congress to control programs by the level of funding, or even kill programs by not funding them. Congress earmarked funds in the *Defense Appropriations Act of 2000* for a Coast Guard Intelligence Program study.

As a point of clarification, authorizing and appropriation are not the same. In Congress, authorizing legislation authorizes the enactment of appropriations. An authorizing measure can establish, continue or modify an agency or program. It also may provide the duties and functions, organizational structure, and responsibilities of agency or program officials.

An appropriations measure provides budget authority to the agency for the purposes specified. This allows federal agencies to incur obligations and authorizes payments to come from the Treasury. Without an appropriation to fund it, the authorization generally means little to an organization, but the authorization is the first step and necessary to get an appropriation.

The SSCI and HPSCI are the authorizers of the IC budget. They forward the budget to the Senate Appropriations Committee (SAC) and House Appropriations Committee (HAC) for appropriation. Since a large portion of the IC budget is within the Department of Defense, both the House Armed Services Committee (HASC) and Senate Armed Services Committee (SASC) have authorization jurisdiction over portions of the IC budget. The HPSCI and SSCI include "crossover" members who can help guide the IC budget through these committees. The HPSCI has at least one crossover member on the House Appropriations Committee, House Armed Services, International Relations, and Judiciary Committees.[24] The SSCI has them from each party on SAC, SASC, foreign relations, and Judiciary committees.[25] The other authorizers often trust SSCI or HPSCI members to verify and validate the classified expenditures, and this acceptance saves time and obviates classified briefings. Three funding streams exist for the IC. They are the National Foreign Intelligence Program (NFIP), Joint Military Intelligence Program (JMIP), and Tactical Intelligence and Related Activities (TIARA). Within the NFIP budget are defense-related and civilian-related programs. General Defense Intelligence Programs (GDIP) funds go through the armed services committees, the intelligence committees, and the SAC/HAC. The funding streams for civilian-

---

23 Richelson, 388.
24 "Crossover" members are required HPSCI and SSCI members who serve on other committees. U.S. Congress, House, Committee On Rules, "108th House Rules," 108th Congress, 1st session, 2003, URL: <http://www.house.gov/rules/RX.htm>, accessed 22 May 2003.
25 U.S. Congress, Senate, *A Resolution Establishing a Select Committee on Intelligence,* 94th Congress, 2nd session, 1976, S. Res. 400, section 2. Cited hereafter as S Res. 400

only CIA, INR, FBI, and Treasury go directly from the HPSCI and SSCI to the HAC/SAC. JMIP and TIARA funding is authorized by the HPSCI but not by the SSCI because the House mandate for the HPSCI includes national and tactical intelligence activities.[26] The SASC authorizes these programs in the Senate. Table 1 summarizes the intricacies of shared jurisdiction over the intelligence budget.

Budget Category	HPSCI	SSCI	ARMED SERVICES	APPRO-PRIATIONS
NFIP (National Foreign Intel Program)				
CIA	YES	YES	NO	YES
Defense NFIP, such as the following:	YES	YES	YES	YES
NGAP (NGA Program)	YES	YES	YES	YES
GDIP (General Defense Intelligence Program– DIA)	YES	YES	YES	YES
CCP (Consolidated Cryptologic Program — NSA)	YES	YES	YES	YES
NRP (Natonal Reconnaissance Program – NRO)	YES	YES	YES	YES
Civilian Intelligence Functions[27] such as:	YES	YES	NO	YES

Continued on next page

26 Smist, 215.
27 HPSCI and SSCI also share jurisdiction with committees that oversee State (Foreign/Int'l Relations); FBI (Judiciary) and Treasury (Finance/Commerce).

Budget Category	HPSCI	SSCI	ARMED SERVICES	APPRO-PRIATIONS
STATE INR (Bureau of Intelligence & Research)	YES	YES	NO	YES
FBI CT (Counter Terrorism)	YES	YES	NO	YES
TREASURY IN	YES	YES	NO	YES
JMIP[28] (Jt Mil Intel Prog — DOD wide) (Programs such as: DCP — Defense Cryptological Program; DIMAP — Defense Imagery Program, Defense Mapping, Charting and Geodesy Program, and DGIAP – Defense General Intel Applications Program)	YES	NO	YES	YES
TIARA (Tactical Intel and Related Activities) (Service Specific)	YES	NO	YES	YES

Figure 1. Shared Jurisdiction Over the Intelligence Budget

Source: Anne Daugherty Miles, "Shared Jurisdiction over the IC Budget," Appendix D in *The Creation of NIMA: Congress's Role as Overseer,* Occasional Paper Number Nine (Washington DC: Joint Military Intelligence College, April 2002), 31. Used with permission.

In terms of oversight, the committee in charge of authorizing the funding stream can exercise the "power of the purse" to choke out a program, earmark or "fence" money, and fund studies. Of course the appropriation of the funds is also required, and this is probably why the SSCI and HPSCI contain crossover members on the powerful appropriations committees.

Organization

Congress has the power to organize the executive branch. Congress, through two separate Hoover commissions in the 1950s, did suggest reorganization

---

28 JMIP was added as a budget category in 1993. In 1996 a MOA was signed between the SSCI and SASC conceding that the SSCI had no formal jurisdiction over either JMIP or TIARA.

guidelines to help the DCI and CIA. Most recently Congress created the Department of Homeland Security. Congress can organize "oversight trips" to examine issues on-site and learn more about programs and organizations.

Reports of Findings and Information

Members can inquire on behalf of their constituents and pressure the IC to divulge information the Community may not have wanted exposed. Congress can pass laws requiring reports of findings and information from executive branch agencies. Freedom of Information Act request reports are one example.

Congressional Oversight of the Intelligence Community

Congress has been involved in intelligence since the beginning of the nation. The Second Continental Congress created the Committee of Secret Correspondence. The members of this committee were charged to gather intelligence from people in England, Ireland, and elsewhere in Europe to help the war effort.[29] It was the most direct involvement ever by any U.S. Congress in actual intelligence gathering and management.

The 1790 authorization of a $40,000 Secret Service Fund by the first Congress, for President George Washington, established the fledgling government's spying capability. The fund grew to one million dollars in three years and was twelve percent of the budget by 1793.[30] Aside from the authorization, additional oversight was lacking. Congress only required that the President certify the funds spent. This allowed the President to conceal who received funds and why. Considerably later, in 1846, President James K. Polk rebuffed a House of Representatives' challenge to the non-disclosure aspects, citing national security concerns.[31] This was the first rebuff of a concerted congressional effort to oversee intelligence spending.

Over the years, through the Civil War, during westward expansion, after acquisition of Spanish colonies, during and following the World Wars, changing needs prodded the Congress into making changes. During World War II, the Congress saw the need for greater involvement in the world community, and recognized the need for more and better intelligence. After the war, there were still further changes with the start of the Cold War and a new political and military environment.

---

29 James S. Van Wagenen, "A Review of Congressional Oversight," *Studies in Intelligence* 1, no. 1 (1997), URL: <http://www.cia.gov/csi/studies/97unclass/wagenen.html>, accessed 21 May 2003; "The Evolution of the U.S. Intelligence Community –An Historic Overview," Government Printing Office n.d URL: <http://www.access.gpo.gov/int/int022.html>, accessed 23 April 2003. Cited hereafter as "Evolution of IC".
30 Van Wagenen, 2; "Evolution of IC," 1.
31 Christopher Andrews, *For the President's Eyes Only* (New York, NY: Harper Collins, 1995), 11-12; Van Wagenen, 3.

Formation and Passage of the *National Security Act of 1947*

The *National Security Act of 1947* vaguely outlined the roles and missions of the CIA, created the position of Director of Central Intelligence, and called into being the National Security Council. The Act clearly established limits on the internal powers of the CIA to prevent the creation of a "Gestapo." Expressly prohibited powers included: "police, subpoena, law enforcement, or internal security functions."[32] This formalized the firewall between national foreign intelligence and law enforcement. Additionally, the law charged the DCI with "protecting intelligence sources and methods from unauthorized disclosure."[33] The inclusion of these provisions demonstrated the concerns of Congress regarding foreign intelligence and forms a basis for later changes and amendments in 1992, 1996, 2001, and 2002.[34] The law enforcement-intelligence divide formalized in this act created a seam between respective organizations that transnational actors and asymmetric opponents[35] seek to exploit. The 1947 law, as amended, also has come to codify IC membership through organizational charter legislation, and most recently has been amended to add new IC members.

Early Oversight

The first Hoover Commission report (1949) was submitted after a congressionally directed investigation into the organization of the executive branch, which included a sub-group evaluating the newly formed CIA. The first report expressed concerns about CIA access to all levels of information possessed by the government. It examined the internal structure and function of CIA and recommended changes and improvements. Placed against the background of the Red Scare and the discovery that Russia had atomic weapons, this commission's report set the stage for congressional support of the IC. It recommended changes to the procurement laws for the DCI, and granted authority to conduct clandestine operations.[36] For the first time, Congress advocated changes for what came to be known as the IC. In operational terms it allowed for simplified contracting and

---

32 "Evolution of IC," 8.

33 "Evolution of IC," 8.

34 In 1992 the *Intelligence Organization Act of 1992* codified IC membership. This act was title VII of the *Intelligence Authorization Act for Fiscal Year 2003*. In 1996 NIMA was created–see Anne Daugherty Miles, *The Creation of NIMA: Congress's Role as Overseer*, Occasional Paper Number Nine (Washington DC: Joint Military Intelligence College, April 2002) for more information. In 2001 the *Intelligence Authorization Act of 2002* added the Coast Guard, and in 2002 the *Homeland Security Act of 2002* added the Department of Homeland Security to the IC.

35 Smuggling of drugs and migrants, terrorist acts, drug violence, and international crime are some common examples.

36 Richard A. Best Jr., and Herbert Boerstling, "Proposals for Intelligence Reorganization, 1949-1996," a report prepared for the Permanent Select Committee on Intelligence, House of Representatives (Washington, DC: Congressional Research Service, Library of Congress, 28 February 1996), 5-6. Cited hereafter as Best and Boerstling, "Proposals for IC Reorganization." Attached as appendix C to U.S. Congress, House, Permanent Select Committee on Intelligence Staff Study, *IC21: Intelligence Community in the 21st Century*, 104th Congress (Washington, DC: GPO, 1996); Mark Lowenthal, *U.S. Intelligence Evolution and Anatomy* 2nd ed. (Washington, DC and Westport, CT: The Center for Strategic and International Studies with Praeger, 1992), 20-21. Cited hereafter as Lowenthal, *U.S. Intelligence;* "Evolution of IC," 9.

procurement. Lifting these restrictions allowed for the CIA to oversee development of the U2 spy plane and other technologies.[37]

A second congressionally mandated study of the executive branch, known as the Second Hoover Commission, took place in 1954. General Mark Clark led a task force on Intelligence Activities. Their findings called for the creation of a Chief of Staff for the DCI and a permanent executive branch commission to oversee the CIA. This would become the Presidential Foreign Intelligence Advisory Board.[38] General Clark's report to Congress "initiated the official use of the term 'Intelligence Community.' Until that time, the U.S. had sought to apply increasing coordination to departmental intelligence efforts, without the concept of a 'community' of departments and agencies."[39]

Specific Congressional Inquiry Committees

The Church Committee

The Church Committee conducted a major oversight investigation of the IC and is itself considered the father of the SSCI. Convened in January of 1975 amid the post-Watergate climate of distrust, disillusionment and disbelief, the Committee to Study Government Operations with Respect to Intelligence Activities was convened to investigate a laundry list of alleged misdeeds.[40] These included: domestic spying activities, interception of U.S. citizen telephone calls, reading private mail, and covert operations including assassinations.[41] The Church Committee initiated a massive shift in congressional conduct of intelligence oversight. Prior to the Church Committee's formation, senior members of the Armed services and Appropriations committees conducted oversight.

> [T]he oversight subcommittees met infrequently, held few formal sessions, and told the Senate and public little. Now, however, the Select Intelligence Committee had been established by the Senate to perform a twofold task: (1) to investigate charges of abuses, and (2) to propose legislative remedies to correct any abuses or deficiencies it might find.[42]

The Committee's work took one year and filled six volumes of findings and recommended actions. These included: the establishment of statutory charters for CIA, NSA, and DIA, strengthening the DCI, outlawing clandestine support

---

37 For more information see John Ranelagh, *The Agency The Rise and Decline of the CIA* revised ed. (New York, NY: Simon and Schuster, 1987), 441-43.

38 Lowenthal, *U.S. Intelligence*, 27; Best and Boerstling, "Proposals for IC Reorganization," 9.

39 Best and Boerstling, "Proposals for IC Reorganization," 9. The term "Intelligence Community" is attributed to: Commission on Organization of the Executive Branch of the Government, A Report to the Congress, *Intelligence Activities*, June 1955, 13.

40 Loch K. Johnson, *A Season of Inquiry: Congress and Intelligence* (Lexington, KY: The University Press of Kentucky, 1985), is the definitive account of the Church Committee.

41 Loch Johnson, 12-13.

42 Smist, 28.

to oppressive regimes, and the formation of a permanent oversight committee in the Senate.[43] The committee recognized reforms made in the IC by the Ford administration.[44] It was regarded as a nonpartisan investigation into alleged IC misdeeds.

Senate Resolution 400, establishing the Senate Select Committee on Intelligence, continued this nonpartisan approach. It gave the majority party just one extra committee member and required a vice chairman from the minority party.[45] The SSCI, spawned by the Church Committee, continued the committee's program of action.[46]

The Pike Committee

The Pike Committee was the second Select Committee on Intelligence formed by the House.[47] The House committee took a "far more adversarial" approach to the conduct of hearings and requests for information.[48] The Pike committee focused more on "the management and organization of the Intelligence Community and proceed[ed] from there to assess how well the community had produced accurate and usable intelligence for decision makers."[49] The recommendations of the committee were leaked to Daniel Schorr and printed in the New York City newspaper *The Village Voice*. The House never approved the Pike committee's findings, although they were officially published.[50]

The Pike Committee report chastised the Intelligence Community's failures to predict the Tet Offensive, the Soviet invasion of Czechoslovakia, the Indian Nuclear bomb test (1974) and other strategic global events. It criticized the procurement and accounting practices of the CIA, recommended the abolition of the DIA, the creation of an Inspector General for CIA, changes to the DCI's responsibilities, strict limitations to interactions between domestic law enforcement agencies and the IC, and the creation of a permanent intelligence oversight committee in the House of Representatives. The Pike Committee Report also included a recommendation to forward National Intelligence Estimates to concerned congressional committees. If adopted it would have designated Congress as a consumer of intelligence.[51] The scandalous leaking of the committee report tainted the credibility of the

---

43 Loch Johnson, 220-226.

44 Executive Order 11905 brought about several of these changes.

45 S Res. 400.

46 14 of 50 Church Committee staffers were held over to form the first SSCI staff.

47 The first Select Committee on Intelligence dissolved after revelations that its chairman, Representative Lucien Nedzi, had knowledge of prior CIA misdeeds. Lowenthal, *U.S. Intelligence*, 41.

48 Best and Boerstling, "Proposals for IC Reorganization," 23.

49 Lowenthal, *U.S. Intelligence*, 42.

50 Best and Boerstling, "Proposals for IC Reorganization," 24. The Pike Committee's report was published on 11 February 1976. U.S. Congress, House, Select Committee on Intelligence, *Recommendations of the Final Report of the House Select Committee on Intelligence*, 94th Congress, 2nd session, House Report 94-833, 11 February 1976.

51 Lowenthal, *U.S. Intelligence*, 44-45; Best and Boerstling, "Proposals for IC Reorganization," 24-25.

Pike Committee's work and doomed the prospects of immediate approval for the committee's recommendations.

The findings of the Pike and Church committees collectively forced the executive branch to reform IC activities. President Ford, anticipating the recommendations of the committees, issued Executive Order 11905. It described the duties and responsibilities of the DCI and members of the IC. It instituted many reforms being considered by Congress, including a ban on assassinations.[52] By initiating changes before Congress could act, President Ford reasserted executive branch primacy over the IC.

Creation of the HPSCI

Gaining some distance from the controversy, the House waited one year before establishing the House Permanent Select Committee on Intelligence (HPSCI). The HPSCI started after the SSCI's first-ever Intelligence Authorization Bill stalled because there was no corresponding committee to receive it in the House of Representatives. Speaker of the House Tip O'Neill proposed a change to the Rules of the House in March of 1977, with the support of the DCI and President, which created the HPSCI in July of 1977.[53] Congress added the HPSCI and SSCI to those committees requiring notification of covert actions under the Hughes Ryan amendment.[54]

Both committees sought to implement legislation addressing the recommendations of the Church and Pike committees. The National Intelligence Organization and Reform Act of 1978 included statutory charters[55] for all IC agencies, recommended the creation of a Director of National Intelligence, and had an extensive list of prohibited activities and notification requirements. John M. Oseth provides a detailed account of the legislation and why it failed to leave committee. One significant law that did pass the 95th Congress was the *Foreign*

---

52 U.S. President, Executive Order 11905, "United States Foreign Intelligence Activities," 18 February 1976, 2, 4, 11-14; "Evolution of the IC," 14.

53 Smist, 214-5.

54 Eight total committees required notification in 1977. L. Britt Snider, *Sharing Secrets with Lawmakers: Congress as a User of Intelligence,* Monograph, Center for the Study of Intelligence (Langley, VA: Central Intelligence Agency, February 1997), 9. This monograph also has a useful chronology of Congressional oversight milestones.

55 Executive Order 11905, signed by President Ford on 18 February 1976, and Executive Order 12036, signed by President Carter on 24 January 1978, included many of the reforms recommended by both committees. The orders preceded Congressional actions and in some cases removed the urgency of reform measure passage. The notification language in EO 12036 was used in the Intelligence Oversight Act of 1980. EO 11905 and EO 12036 are both substantial oversight initiatives enacted by the President. However, the focus of this publication is on congressional oversight actions. For further information on these Executive Orders see John M. Oseth, *Regulating U.S. Intelligence Operations. A study in Definition of the National Interest* (Lexington, KY: The University Press of Kentucky, 1985) 91-100, 112-122; and Lowenthal, *U. S. Intelligence,* 43, 52, 68, and 107.

Intelligence Surveillance Act of 1978, which formed the legal basis for electronic surveillance inside U.S. borders.[56]

Formation and Passage of the *Intelligence Oversight Act of 1980*

The *Intelligence Oversight Act of 1980* included provisions requiring the heads of the intelligence agencies to keep oversight committees "fully and currently informed" of their activities including "any significant anticipated intelligence activities."[57] It also reduced the prior notification requirements for covert operations to just the HPSCI and SSCI, solidifying their primacy as intelligence community oversight committees. Additional rules for safeguarding the information those committees received were included in the legislation.[58] This codified the requirement to keep Congress informed, making failure to do so a violation of the law.

The Iran-Contra Scandal

After learning about the Reagan Administration National Security Council Staff's orchestration of arms sales to Iran in return for the release of hostages held in Lebanon, and the subsequent diversion of these "third party" funds to Nicaraguan Contras, on 6 January 1987 the Senate formed the Select Committee on Secret Military Assistance to Iran and the Nicaraguan Opposition.[59] The House followed suit the next day, forming the House Select Committee to Investigate Covert Arms Transactions with Iran.[60] The failure to notify the HPSCI and SSCI of the covert arms sales to Iran violated the *Intelligence Oversight Act of 1980.* The Diversion of funds to aid the contras violated the fourth Boland Amendment.[61] This was the first serious breach of these recently established Congressional oversight arrangements by the executive branch and the IC. The House and Senate formed

---

56 Best and Boerstling, "Proposals for IC Reorganization," 26; John M. Oseth, *Regulating U.S. Intelligence Operations: A study in Definition of the National Interest* (Lexington, KY: The University Press of Kentucky. 1985), 108-111.

57 U.S. Congress, House, Permanent Select Committee on Intelligence, *Intelligence Oversight Act of 1980,* House Report 96-1153, 96th Cong., 2 session. (1980). Cited by John M. Oseth, *Regulating U.S. Intelligence Operations. A study in Definition of the National Interest* (Lexington, KY: The University Press of Kentucky. 1985), 147.

58 Oseth, 147.

59 U.S. Congress, House, House Select Committee to Investigate Covert Arms Transactions with Iran and Senate Select Committee on Secret Military Assistance to Iran and the Nicaraguan Opposition, *Report of the Congressional Committees Investigating the Iran-Contra Affair,* 100th Congress, 1st session, 1987, H. Rept. 100-433, S. Rept. 100-216, xv. Cited hereafter as the *Iran-Contra Report.*

60 *Iran-Contra Report,* xv. This is a cursory treatment of an extremely complicated event. In the context of this publication it illustrates congressional response to scandal and the genesis of future reform efforts. The *Iran-Contra Report* presents the Congressional Investigation's findings. The *Report of the President's Special Review Board* was published as *The Tower Commission Report* (New York: Bantam Books, and Random House, 1987). Both reports and numerous books examine the scandal at length.

61 Lowenthal, *U.S. Intelligence,* 79-80.

two separate investigative committees then later merged them into one.[62] After several weeks of public testimony, the Committees recommended the creation of a CIA IG office and the tightening of oversight and covert action reporting requirements.[63] The findings led to the resignation of several high-level NSC staffers, and criminal charges against NSC staff members, CIA employees, and a former Secretary of Defense.[64]

Passage of the *Intelligence Organization Act of 1992*

This act for the first time codified IC membership.[65] In his tome on oversight, Smist credits the passage of this act to the leadership of then-SSCI Chairman, Senator David Boren, and the hard work of SSCI General Counsel, L. Britt Snider. After the Cold War and first Persian Gulf War victories, Chairman Boren had tasked Snider to "come up with a bill that was 'bold and provocative,' to stimulate the executive branch into thinking imaginatively about intelligence reorganization."[66] In 1992, Snider drafted charter legislation for the FBI, CIA, State and Defense Departments. Chairman Boren and Snider addressed individual agency concerns and White House objections on a case-by-case basis. DCI Robert Gates gave his support to the changes in August of 1992 and the law passed.[67]

At the time of passage the members of the "Intelligence Community" included: the Office of the DCI, The National Intelligence Council, CIA, DIA, NSA, Central Imagery Organization (CIO) (which would become part of NIMA), the NRO, specialized national reconnaissance elements of DOD, the Bureau of Intelligence and Research of the Department of State and the intelligence elements of: the Department of Energy, FBI, Department of Treasury, and the Army, the Navy, the Air Force, and the Marine Corps.[68] Also in the bill was a provision which allowed entry into the IC of "such other elements of any other department or agency as may be designated by the President, or designated jointly by the Director of Central Intelligence and the head of the department or agency concerned."[69] This asserted the executive branch's power to shape the IC. The SSCI committee report summarized the impact of title VII by writing that it "provide[d] for the first time in law a comprehensive statement of the responsibilities and authorities of the agencies and officials of the U.S. intelligence community."[70]

---

62 Indicative of increased cooperation and experience of the HPSCI and SSCI, the committee investigating the terrorist attacks of 11 September 2001 was formed jointly from the onset.

63 *Iran-Contra Report* 423-27; Smist, 264,266; Lowenthal, *U.S. Intelligence,* 81.

64 "Evolution of the IC," 17-18.

65 Passed as Title VII of the *Intelligence Authorization Act for Fiscal Year 1993.* Another provision of this act allowed the Defense Intelligence College (JMIC's predecessor) to award academic degrees.

66 Smist, 286. Smist attributes the bold and provocative quote to an anonymous interview.

67 Smist, 286.

68 Title VII, section 3 of Public Law 102-496, *Intelligence Authorization Act for Fiscal Year 1993.* Cited hereafter as FY93 Intel Auth Act.

69 FY93 Intel Auth Act.

70 U.S. Congress, Senate, Select Committee on Intelligence, *Special Report,* 103rd Congress, 1st session, 18 March 1993, 3. Quoted in Smist, 286.

The fiscal year (FY) 1993 bill was the last Intelligence Authorization Bill passed under Boren's six-year chairmanship of the SSCI. Chairman Boren used previous Intelligence Authorization bills to shape and reform the IC. The FY 1990 bill had created an independent Inspector General for CIA. Senate Resolution 2834, the initial Intelligence Authorization Bill for FY 1991, was the first-ever Intelligence Authorization Bill vetoed. "This unprecedented action was necessitated in the President's judgment by congressional attempts to reform, in the wake of the Iran-Contra affair, the way in which covert actions are conceived, reported and implemented."[71] President George H. Bush's objection was to the statutory definition of covert action, specifically its impact on foreign governments and third parties.[72]

The subsequent FY 1991 bill, without the objectionable language, passed in August of 1991.[73] It succeeded in changing how covert actions were reported and approved by Congress. "Chairman Boren thus is the person primarily responsible for enacting the legislative reform proposals of both the Church and Iran Contra committees."[74] According to a Smist interview of a senior staffer who wanted to remain anonymous, "the authorization process was used to pass substantial legislation. *It's a matter of convenience. That's the bill that has to go through. The executive branch will want it. It is harder to veto than free-standing legislation.*"[75] A decade later, the Coast Guard entered the IC thorough a provision in the *Intelligence Appropriations Bill for Fiscal Year 2002.*

Aspin-Brown

Formally known as the Commission on the Roles and Capabilities of the U.S. Intelligence Community, the Aspin-Brown Commission was sanctioned by section 904 of the *Intelligence Authorization Act for Fiscal Year 1995* (P.L. 103-359). The commission's mandate was to review "the efficacy and appropriateness of the activities" of the IC and make recommendations "considered advisable."[76] The Aspin-Brown report recommended the expansion of IC missions to include support "countering illicit activities abroad which threaten U.S. interests, including terrorism, narcotics trafficking," and other transnational threats.[77] The commission

---

71 William E. Conner, *Intelligence Oversight; the Controversy Behind The FY 1991 Intelligence Authorization Act The Intelligence Profession Series Number Eleven* (McLean, VA: The Association of Former Intelligence Officers, 1993), 1. Conner examined and provided additional insight into the power struggle between the President and Congress over the reform aspects of this act.

72 Conner, 29-30.

73 Conner, 35.

74 Smist, 287.

75 Smist, 276. Quote attributed to a "senior committee staffer" in a confidential interview. Emphasis added. President Bush's earlier veto was made possible because funding for the IC had been appropriated by the FY 1991 Defense Appropriations Act which President Bush signed on 5 November 1990. Funding for the IC was appropriated but not authorized, see Conner 29-37.

76 Commission on the Roles and Missions of the United States Intelligence Community, *Preparing for the 21st Century, an appraisal of U.S. Intelligence, Washington*, DC: GPO, 1 March 1996, xv. Available at URL: <http://www.access.gpo.gov/su_docs/dpos/epubs/int/pdf/report.html>. Cited hereafter as Aspin-Brown report.

77 Aspin-Brown report, xvii, 37.

called for greater cooperation between Law Enforcement and Intelligence communities, noted the overlapping responsibilities and that the "internecine squabbles between agencies seriously undermined the country's ability to combat global crime in an effective manner and must be ended."[78] Other recommendations included the need for closer interaction between the IC and policymakers, the need to maintain strong "right sized" intelligence capabilities, adopt a more effective budget structure and process, improve intelligence analysis, and increase international cooperation.[79] HPSCI Chairman and sponsor of the Coast Guard IC membership provision, Representative Porter Goss (R-FL), was a member of the Aspin-Brown Commission.[80]

IC21

IC21 was a comprehensive study by the HPSCI staff that prescribed numerous adjustments to the IC. It represented the evolution of oversight, as it recommended creating a position of DDCI for Community Management; shifting more budgetary control to the DCI; re-organizing the IC according to mission, limiting the length of service for the DCI, reevaluating intelligence and LE collection requirements, as well as encouraging collaborative technology development and research functions.[81] IC21 was important because it represented the HPSCI going beyond the traditional concepts of oversight, extending its reach into management recommendations. Even though the proposals presented weren't immediately adopted, the shapers of this policy were later in positions to make some of the recommended changes.[82]

The Coast Guard's entry into the IC was a significant test case for Congressional oversight of the IC because it was a HPSCI initiative accomplished against the recommendation of the DDCI for Community Management. CGIP entry was engineered by the Congress and enacted through amending the *National Security Act of 1947*. Some sources interviewed saw this as one method to move the IC away from the Cold War and advance some of the dismissed IC21 and Aspin-Brown initiatives.[83]

---

78 Aspin-Brown, 38.

79 Aspin-Brown, xv-xxv.

80 Aspin-Brown, G-2.

81 U.S. Congress, House, Permanent Select Committee on Intelligence, Staff Study, *IC21: Intelligence Community in the 21st Century,* 104th Congress, 2nd session (Washington, DC: GPO, 1996), 10-13, 15, 35, 272-273. Cited hereafter as *IC21.*

82 Mark Lowenthal was HPSCI staff director of the study and then an Assistant DCI for Analysis. Congressman Porter Goss, (R) FL, and Congresswoman Nancy Pelosi (D) CA, were HPSCI members when IC21 was released. Congressman Goss was HPSCI Chairman and Congresswoman Pelosi Ranking Democrat when the *Intelligence Appropriations Act for Fiscal Year 2002* passed.

83 Since they were commenting on other people's unstated motivations, these sources preferred to remain anonymous. However, more than one source referred to this as one possible motivation.

Origins of IC Membership

Intelligence is often referred to as the second-oldest profession. Several of the institutions that make up the IC can trace their foundation and history to the very beginning of the nation and some even predate it. Many organizations claim origins that predate their creation under the present name, CIA as OSS for example. The intent here is to track how the current IC members were formed, by whose initiative,[84] and to summarize how each formally entered the IC. The following section focuses on when the organization became chartered under that name and how. It also tracks the evolution of membership and "Community" creation, thereby providing a means of gauging congressional involvement.

There are two types of IC members. The agencies for which every component is part of the IC are members in their entirety; those for whom only the national foreign intelligence component of that agency is part of the IC, are intelligence component members.

Members in their entirety

The Central Intelligence Agency (CIA) was created in 1947 with the signing of the National Security Act by President Truman.[85] At the time, it was the only civilian intelligence agency charged with a national mission. The Federal Bureau of Investigation maintained sole responsibility for domestic and counterintelligence matters.

The Defense Intelligence Agency (DIA) was formed in 1961 to provide a national focus for Army, Navy,[86] and Air Force intelligence and to reduce redundancy. Prior to DIA's creation, each armed service collected, analyzed and disseminated its own intelligence and provided separate estimates to the Secretary of Defense. In 1960 President Eisenhower appointed a joint study group to "determine better ways of effectively organizing the nation's military intelligence activities."[87] Based on that study group's recommendations, Secretary of Defense Robert S. McNamara created the Defense Intelligence Agency. He tasked the Joint Chiefs of Staff (JCS) with devising an integration plan. "The JCS completed this assignment by July, and published DoD Directive 5105.21, "Defense Intelligence

---

84 Mark Lowenthal, *U.S. Intelligence Evolution and Anatomy* 2nd ed. (Washington, DC and Westport, CT: The Center for Strategic and International Studies with Praeger, 1992) is a very good collective IC history, while the sources cited here focus more on individual agencies.

85 *Intelligence Community Homepage*, "Members of the IC: the Central Intelligence Agency," URL: <http://www.intelligence.gov/1-members_cia.shtml>, accessed 23 May 2003; Michael Warner, *Central Intelligence: Origin and Evolution* (Washington, DC: Center for the Study of Intelligence, CIA, 2001), 4-5. Warner provides a brief but through examination of the historical background of the CIA's creation. This work includes several declassified documents and provides an excellent start for people researching the evolution of the CIA.

86 To include Marine Corps intelligence.

87 DIA Homepage, "History- Intro," URL: < http://www.dia.mil/History/40years/intro. html>, accessed 23 May 2003; A. Denis Clift, *Clift Notes Intelligence & the Nation's Security*, First Edition (Washington, DC: Joint Military Intelligence College, 2000), 13-15.

Agency" on 1 August, effective 1 October 1961."[88] The DIA was formed by the Secretary of Defense and entered the existing IC, replacing the JCS intelligence component.[89]

At nearly the same time, Defense Secretary McNamara formally established, on 6 September 1961, the National Reconnaissance Program. The program had responsibility for "all satellite and overflight reconnaissance projects whether overt or covert."[90] The consolidation and reorganization of a civilian office of the Undersecretary of the Air Force and other imagery programs run by CIA and the Office of Naval Intelligence became the National Reconnaissance Office (NRO). These programs were transferred by internal memorandums and in the CIA's case the NRO charter was signed by Deputy Director of Central Intelligence General Charles Pearre Cabell.[91] The new organization was formed in secrecy; and the name NRO remained classified for the next 21 years.[92]

The National Security Agency, another secretive IC member, was created by President Truman. At the recommendation of a presidentially impaneled committee chaired by George A. Brownell, President Truman signed an executive memorandum that determined that "cryptology was a 'national asset'" and made the Secretary of Defense the executive agent for Signals Intelligence. In that executive memorandum he created the National Security Agency "with nothing more than a signature" on 4 November 1952.[93]

During his confirmation hearings, DCI nominee John Deutch promised to improve the efficiency of imagery intelligence "by managing imagery in a manner similar to the National Security Agency's organization for signals intelligence."[94] When Deutch became DCI, eight separate imagery entities, most within the existing Community, were combined to form the National Imagery and Mapping Agency (NIMA). Congress created NIMA on 1 October 1996 by the *National Imagery and Mapping Agency Act of 1996*, which was part of the FY97 Department of Defense

---

88 *Intelligence Community Homepage*, "Members of the IC: the Defense Intelligence Agency," URL: <http://www.intelligence.gov/1-members_dia.shtml>, accessed 23 May 2003.

89 Deane J. Allen, Brian G. Shellum eds., *Defense Intelligence Agency at the Creation 1961-1965* (Washington: DC, DIA History Office, Defense Intelligence Agency, 2002) xix-xxi. This work is the definitive study of the creation of DIA and contains many primary source documents.

90 R. Cargill Hill, "The NRO at Forty: Ensuring Global Information Supremacy," *NRO 40th Anniversary webpage*, n.d. 2 URL: <http:www.nro.gov/40thann/NROHistory.pdf >, accessed 23 May 2003.

91 Hill, 3-4.

92 Representative George Brown was forced to resign from the HPSCI for remarks delivered on the floor of the House that disclosed the missions and capabilities of NRO satellites and used the agencies name, see Smist, 319. The Agency was declassified in 1992 during the debate over the FY1993 Intelligence Authorization Bill.

93 Nation Security Agency, *National Security Agency 1952-2002: Cryptologic Excellence: Yesterday, Today, Tomorrow* (50th anniversary monograph) (Ft Meade, MD: National Security Agency, n.d.) 13. URL: <http://www.nsa.gov/images/50th_brochure.pdf>, accessed 23 May 2003; James Bamford, *The Puzzle Palace, Inside the National Security Agency, America's Most Secret Intelligence Organization* (New York: Penguin Books, 1983), 15.

94 U.S. Congress, Senate, Select Committee on Intelligence, Confirmation Hearings of John Deutch, 104th Congress, 1st session, 26 April 1995.

Authorization bill.[95] Miles provides a detailed account of the role Congress played in creating the agency. Unlike the Coast Guard, the majority of NIMA's components were part of the IC, and the creation of the organization was DCI John Deutch's initiative, backed by the Chairman of the Joint Chiefs of Staff and the Secretary of Defense.[96]

After World War II President Truman ordered the dissolution of the Office of Strategic Services (OSS). The Research and Analysis Component of the OSS shifted to the State Department on 1 October 1945, where it became the Bureau of Intelligence and Research (INR).[97] The Bureau provides all-source analysis and evaluates policy decisions for the Department of State but does not collect intelligence.[98]

Component members

For the remaining IC members, only their intelligence components are members of the IC. For example, only the intelligence component of the Department of Energy is an IC member, not the entire department. This is an important distinction reflecting the fact that most members of the armed forces, or employees of the Treasury or Energy Departments, are not engaged in espionage or intelligence work. More importantly, the FBI special agents, customs officials, and DEA agents performing their traditional duties are acting as law enforcement officials, and are *not* agents of the Intelligence Community. Only those personnel assigned to the national foreign intelligence elements of these agencies are part of the IC.

The functional separation between the national foreign intelligence components and the law enforcement components of the same agency is maintained by the concept of a "firewall." For the Coast Guard, the separation of its national foreign intelligence mission from its law enforcement mission was a major concern of the IC. Only the national intelligence element of the Coast Guard is a member of the IC. The boarding officers and inspectors of the Coast Guard are acting as enforcement officers, *not* intelligence agents.

Attorney General Charles Bonaparte during the Theodore Roosevelt administration created the FBI in 1908.[99] Prior to creation of the FBI on 27 May

---

95 Anne Daugherty Miles, Ph.D., *The Creation of the National Imagery and Mapping Agency: Congress's Role as Overseer,* Occasional Paper Number Nine (Washington, DC: Joint Military Intelligence College, 2001), 22. *DoD directive 5105.60* establishing NIMA within DoD as approved by Congress was signed 1 October 1996; *Intelligence Community Homepage*, "Members of the IC: the National Imagery and Mapping Agency," URL: <http://www.intelligence.gov/1-members_nima.shtml>, accessed 23 May 2003.

96 Miles, 1, Appendix F.

97 Lowenthal, *U.S. Intelligence,* 13.

98 Despite being only a component of the Department of State, INR is named separately in the *National Security Act of 1947.*

99 Federal Bureau of Investigation Homepage, Library and References Section, "History of the FBI; Origins 1908-1910," URL: <http://www.fbi.gov/libref/historic/history/origins.htm>, accessed 27 May 2003. Cited hereafter as FBI Origins.

1908, Congress had enacted a law preventing the Department of Justice from using Secret Service operatives. Bonaparte responded by hiring his own special agents within the Department of Justice, and this force became known as the FBI.[100]

World War I saw the advent of the first intelligence-related missions for the FBI. "As a result of the war, the Bureau acquired responsibility for the Espionage, Selective Service, and Sabotage Acts, and assisted the Department of Labor by investigating enemy aliens."[101] Leading up to and during World War II, the Bureau continued to investigate suspected acts of espionage and sabotage. "In 1939 and again in 1943, Presidential directives had authorized the FBI to carry out investigations of threats to national security."[102] The Cold War and fears of nuclear and technological transfer placed more demands on the FBI's counterintelligence mission. In 1982, after the FBI and Drug Enforcement Administration joined the IC, the FBI represented DEA interests within the IC, and DEA was no longer a "named" member of the IC.[103] The FBI remains the principal domestic counterintelligence agency in the IC at this time.

The Department of Treasury's Office of Intelligence Support was preceded by the Office of National Security (ONS), which had been set up by Treasury Secretary Douglas Dillon in 1961 to connect Treasury with the National Security Council.[104]

The Department of Energy's intelligence program originated in the Atomic Energy Commission (AEC), which was formed by the Atomic Energy Act signed by President Truman on 1 August 1946. The act transferred to the AEC control of the U.S. Army Corps of Engineers Manhattan District, which had been used to develop the first atomic bombs. Shortly after its formation, the AEC was tasked to provide specialized analysis of possible atomic weapons programs in the Soviet Union.[105] The specialized scientific knowledge needed to track other countries' weapons program progress resided uniquely within the AEC, thereby forcing its entry. It was an inclusion based on specialty knowledge and need.

---

100 FBI Origins.

101 Federal Bureau of Investigation Homepage, Library and References Section, "History of the FBI; Early Days 1910-1921," URL: <http://www.fbi.gov/libref/historic/history/earlydays.htm>, accessed 27 May 2003.

102 Federal Bureau of Investigation Homepage, Library and References Section, "History of the FBI; Postwar America 1945-1960," URL: <http://www.fbi.gov/libref/historic/history/earlydays. htm>, accessed 27 May 2003.

103 Drug Enforcement Administration Homepage, DEA history section, "Concurrent Jurisdiction with the FBI (1982)," URL: <http://www.dea.gov/pubs/history/deahistory_03.htm#5>, accessed 30 May 2003.

104 *Intelligence Community Homepage*, "Members of the IC: Department of the Treasury: Office of Intelligence Support," URL: <http://www.intelligence.gov/1-members_treasury.shtml>, accessed 23 May 2003

105 Alice L. Buck, *A History of the Atomic Energy Commission* (Washington, DC: U.S. Department of Energy, 1983) 1, 26. URL: <http://tis.eh.doe.gov/workstation/archives/fa118.pdf>, accessed 23 May 2003; *Intelligence Community Homepage*, "Members of the IC: Department of Energy: Office of Intelligence," URL: <http://www.intelligence.gov/1-members_energy.shtml>, accessed 23 May 2003.

The Department of Homeland Security's Information Analysis and Infra-structure Protection (DHS IA/IP) division was legislated into the IC with the 25 November 2002 passage of the *Homeland Security Act of 2002*. Section 201 (h) of the law amended the *National Security Act of 1947* for the second time in as many years by adding the Intelligence "elements" of the Department of Homeland Security.[106]

Military components

Military intelligence components have existed since the birth of the nation. Commanders in combat have always relied on some form of intelligence. The true date of the creation of these IC members is the date of their service's creation, 1775 for most. All military intelligence components evolved and were not created at once. As technology and demands increased so did the intelligence functions of the Armed Services.[107] The evolution of U.S. Army intelligence offers a prime example.

Given the battlefield commander's constant need for intelligence, the Military Intelligence branch of the Army traces its origins to Knowlton's raiders, a reconnaissance and cavalry unit established by General Washington in 1776.[108] The constant need for battlefield information ensured that a Military Intelligence component existed in some form during every war and would evolve as needed. Early Army aerial reconnaissance by balloon during the Civil war is one example of this evolution.

The U.S. Air Force Intelligence component can trace its origins to the Army Signal Corps, which flew the first airplanes and conducted aerial trench surveys in World War I. The Air Force Security Group was formally established in the Directorate of Intelligence, HQ USAF, on 23 June 1948, with a cadre of eleven officers and some clerical enlisted personnel on loan from the Army Security Agency.[109] It has since evolved into the Air Intelligence Agency. Other USAF intelligence components were originally part of the U.S. Army Air Corps, and transferred when the USAF was created as part of the *National Security Act of 1947*.

---

106 *Homeland Security Act of 2002*, Public law 107-296. U.S. Congress, 107th Congress, 2nd Session. Sec 201(h).

107 Harold C. Relyea, *Evolution and Organization of Intelligence Activities in the United States* (Laguna Hills, CA: Aegean Park Press, n.d) provides an extensive and comprehensive overview of the early years of military intelligence and the IC. It was originally published in 1976 by the Church Committee as "The Evolution and Organization of the Federal Intelligence Function: A Brief Overview (1776-1975)."

108 US Army Intelligence Center Fort Huachuca, *A Brief History of US Army Intelligence* (Fort Huachuca, AZ: Fort Huachuca Museums, n.d) 3. URL: <http://usaic.hua.army.mil/History/ PDFS/briefmi.pdf>, accessed 23 May 2003. The highest individual award given for excellence in U.S. Army Intelligence is known as the Knowlton Award.

109 US Air Force Air Intelligence Agency, "History retrospective," Air Intelligence Agency homepage URL: <http://aia.lackland.af.mil/homepages/ho/40s-2.cfm>, accessed 23 May 2003.

U.S. Naval intelligence was formalized at the time when America was becoming an industrial power. "Established in 1882, Naval Intelligence was formed to take advantage of the burgeoning technology employed by foreign navies."[110] Keeping pace with the transition to steel hulls and steam power required a network of naval attachés dispatched worldwide and especially to naval powers. The Office of Naval Intelligence (ONI) grew to help the Navy adapt to changing technology.[111] Marine Corps intelligence has functioned under the Department of the Navy, but has existed tactically since the creation of the Corps in 1775. The Marine Corps became a member of the IC "in recognition of its special global tactical missions."[112]

IC MEMBER	IAC, 1947-58	USCIB, 1946-58	EO 11905, 1976	EO 12036, 1978	EO 12333, 1981	Intl Organization Act 1992
CIA	YES	YES	YES	YES	YES	YES
NSA	NO	YES	YES	YES	YES	YES
NRO	NO	NO	YES*	YES*	YES*	YES
DIA	NO	NO	YES	YES	YES	YES
INR	YES	YES	YES	YES	YES	YES
Agencies that formed NIMA	NO	NO	YES*	YES*	YES	YES
FBI	NO	YES	YES	YES	YES	YES
Dept of Treasury	NO	NO	YES	YES	YES	YES
Dept of Energy	YES (AEC)	NO	YES	YES	YES	YES
Army Intel	YES	YES	YES	YES	YES	YES
USAF Intel	YES	YES	YES	YES	YES	YES
USN Intel	YES	YES	YES	YES	YES	YES

Continued on next page

110 *Intelligence Community Homepage*, "Members of the IC: U.S. Navy Intelligence," URL: <http://www.intelligence.gov/1-members_navy.shtml>, accessed 23 May 2003; Office of Naval Intelligence "Our History," ONI homepage URL: <http://www.nmic.navy.mil/history.htm>, accessed 23 May 2003.Cited hereafter as ONI history.
111 ONI history.
112 Scott D. Breckinridge, *The CIA and the U.S. Intelligence System* (Boulder, CO: Westview Press, 1986), 46.

IC Member	Date Established	Method of Establishment	People Responsible
CIA	18 Sept 1947	National Security Act	President Truman w/ 80th Congress
NSA	4 Nov 1952	Executive memorandum	President Truman
NRO	6 Sept 1961	DOD directive	Secretary of Defense, McNamara
DIA	1 Oct 1961	DOD directive	Secretary of Defense, McNamara
INR	1 Oct 1945	Executive Memorandum	President Truman
NIMA	1 Oct 1996	FY1997 Defense Authorization Bill	President Clinton w/ 104th Congress
FBI	1908	DOJ internal document	Attorney General Bonaparte
Dept of Treasury	1961	DOT internal document	Treasury Secretary Douglas Dillon
Dept of Energy	1946	Atomic Energy Act	President Truman w/ 79th Congress
DHS IA/IP	25 Nov 2002	Homeland Sec Act	President G. W. Bush w/ 107th Congress
US Army Intel	1775	Existed tactically	General Washington, Continental Congress
USAF, AIA	1947 1948	Existed in U.S. Army Air Corps, internal doctrine.	President Truman w/ 80th Congress
USN, ONI	1775 1798 1882	Existed tactically Reestablished Internal document	Continental CongressPres Adams w/ 5th Congress, Sec of the Navy
USMC	1775	Existed tactically	Continental Congress
USCG	1790 28 Dec 2001	Existed tactically FY 2002 Intel Auth Act	Pres Washington w/1stCongress Pres Bush w/ 107th Congress

Figure 2. IC Membership Origins

Source: compiled by author, LCDR Kevin Wirth, USCG.

The four primary military components existed tactically and grew to have strategic missions. All have historically been classified as Intelligence Community members. Of the remaining ten organizations, six were created by the executive branch through a Presidential or Agency decree and the four others (CIA, NIMA, USCG, and DHS IA/IP) were created or made part of the IC by legislation. Table 2 tracks the date and method of creation for all named IC members, starting with members in entirety component members, and lastly military members.

Community?

The term "Intelligence Community" was neither included nor defined in the original *National Security Act of 1947*. General Mark Clark first coined the term in a 1955 *Intelligence Activities* report to Congress.[113] The membership of the Intelligence Advisory Committee (IAC) formed in 1947 probably best represented the initial community.[114] Members included "the DCI as chairman and representatives from the Departments of State, Army, Navy, Air Force, the Joint Chiefs of Staff, and the Atomic Energy Commission."[115] The main function of this body was coordination and the power of the DCI was very limited.

Another early advisory commission was the United States Communications Intelligence Board (USCIB). Formed in 1946, the principal role of USCIB was to advise the Secretary of Defense on Communications Intelligence issues. Members of the USCIB included: "Secretaries of Defense and State, the Director of the FBI, and representatives of the Army, Navy, Air Force, and CIA….Although the DCI sat on the board, he had no vote."[116] At the recommendation of the President's Board of Consultants on Foreign Intelligence Activities,[117] the IAC and USCIB merged to form the United States Intelligence Board (USIB) in 1958.[118] The USIB served as a forum for coordination and for "various members to advance their interests."[119]

U.S. Intelligence Board membership provided one method of accessing IC membership. Between 1958 and 1976, the U.S. "Intelligence Community" changed with the creation of new members and agencies. Along with the merger of the IAC and USCIB, the FBI and National Security Agency (NSA) were added. The FBI was restricted to counterintelligence matters and the Director of NSA served as a technical advisor on the U.S. Intelligence Board.[120] With the creation of DIA, the Joint Chiefs of Staff ceased attending. The Atomic Energy Commission was absorbed by the Department of Energy and the Drug Enforcement Administration

---

113 Best and Boerstling, "Proposals for IC Reorganization," 9.

114 The IAC appeared as a coordinating body to "establish intelligence requirements among Departments." U.S. Congress, Senate, Select Committee to Study Governmental Operations with Respect to Intelligence Activities, *Final Report of Select Committee to Study Governmental Operations with Respect to Intelligence Activities; Book I Foreign and Military Intelligence*, 94th Congress, 2nd session, 26 April 1976, S. Rept 94-755, 103. Cited hereafter as the *Church Committee Report, Book I*.

115 National Security Council Intelligence Directive No 1., 12 December 1947, cited in U.S. Congress, Senate, Select Committee to Study Governmental Operations with Respect to Intelligence Activities, *Final Report of Select Committee to Study Governmental Operations with Respect to Intelligence Activities; Book I Foreign and Military Intelligence*, 94th Congress, 2nd session, 26 April 1976, S. Rept 94-755, 71.

116 *Church Committee Report*, Book I, 114.

117 This was a predecessor to the Presidential Foreign Intelligence Advisory Board (PFIAB).

118 Breckinridge, 42-43.

119 Breckinridge, 43.

120 Breckinridge, 45.

(DEA), created in 1973, was absorbed by the Department of Justice and represented within the IC by the FBI.[121]

On 18 February 1976, President Ford in Executive Order 11905 (EO 11905) defined the membership of the Intelligence Community for the first time. In section 2 paragraph b, the IC is presented as the:

> Central Intelligence Agency; National Security Agency; Defense Intelligence Agency; Special offices within the Department of Defense for the collection of specialized intelligence through reconnaissance programs within the Defense Department [NRO and NIMA components]; Intelligence components of the military services; Intelligence elements of the Federal Bureau of investigation, Intelligence element of the Department of State, Intelligence element of the Department of the Treasury; and Intelligence element of the Energy Research and Development Administration.[122]

In January of 1978, President Carter issued Executive Order 12036 (EO 12036), which replaced EO 11905. In EO 12036 he included all the members listed above and added the Drug Enforcement Administration, and the Staff of the Office of the DCI.[123] Subsequently President Reagan superseded EO 12306 with his own Executive Order 12333 (EO 12333).

The Executive Orders of both President Carter and President Ford used "intelligence components of the military services" without further definition. The Coast Guard is included in the United States Code definitions of Armed Force[124] and 14 U.S.C. § 1 states the Coast Guard "shall be a military service and branch of the United States at all times."[125]

EO 12333 is the cognizant executive order on intelligence activities. President Reagan signed the order on 4 December 1981. It contributed greatly to the DCI's power by giving the DCI full responsibility for "production and dissemination of national foreign intelligence," designating the DCI "as the primary intelligence advisor to the President, and NSC on national foreign intelligence" and allowing the DCI to task non-CIA intelligence agencies.[126] The IC defined in E.O. 12333 removed the DEA as a named member but retained all other members previously defined. It also listed the military components by name, effectively barring entry to the IC for the Coast Guard as a military service and armed force.

---

121 Breckinridge, 45, 46. The Director of National Intelligence and the U.S. Attorney General on 17 February 2006 designated the Drug Enforcement Administration as the 16th member of the IC.
122 U.S. President, Executive Order 11905, "United States Foreign Intelligence Activities," 18 February 1976, 2.
123 U.S. President, Executive Order 12036, "United States Foreign Intelligence Activities," 24 January 1978, 21.
124 10 U.S.C. § 101 includes Coast Guard in the definition of armed force.
125 14 U.S.C. § 1.
126 U.S. President, Executive Order 12333, "United States Intelligence Activities," 4 December 1981. Section 1.5

IC MEMBER	IAC, 1947-58	USCIB, 1946-58	EO 11905, 1976	EO 12036, 1978	EO 12333, 1981	Intl Organization Act 1992
CIA	YES	YES	YES	YES	YES	YES
NSA	NO	YES	YES	YES	YES	YES
NRO	NO	NO	YES*	YES*	YES*	YES
DIA	NO	NO	YES	YES	YES	YES
INR	YES	YES	YES	YES	YES	YES
Agencies that formed NIMA	NO	NO	YES*	YES*	YES	YES
FBI	NO	YES	YES	YES	YES	YES
Dept of Treasury	NO	NO	YES	YES	YES	YES
Dept of Energy	YES (AEC)	NO	YES	YES	YES	YES
Army Intel	YES	YES	YES	YES	YES	YES
USAF Intel	YES	YES	YES	YES	YES	YES
USN Intel	YES	YES	YES	YES	YES	YES
USMC Intel	NO	NO	YES	YES	YES	YES
Others	JCS	None	None	DEA	None	None

Figure 3. Evolution of IC Membership

Source: compiled by author, LCDR Kevin Wirth, USCG.

*Agencies were not named but covered under "Special offices within the Department of Defense for the collection of specialized intelligence through reconnaissance programs."– EO 11905

One other method of defining the IC would be by funding or function. The Coast Guard Intelligence Program was supported for years with funding and facilities before formal inclusion in 2001. Other entities receive some funding and assistance, but remain unnamed members of the IC. Additionally some collection entities provide information to the IC without being named. By mission or funding the Coast Guard could have been considered a member of the IC prior to passage of the *Intelligence Authorization Act of Fiscal Year 2002.*

Figure 3 summarizes the evolution of IC membership by listing the members of the Intelligence Advisory Council (IAC) (1947) and U.S. Communications Intelligence Board (USCIB) (1946-1958), along with agencies listed by Executive Orders 11905 (1976) and 12333 (1981), and the Intelligence Organization Act of 1992.

HOW THE CGIP ENTERED THE INTELLIGENCE COMMUNITY

By what process did the Coast Guard become a member of the Intelligence Community? Beginning with initial congressional interest in the Coast Guard Intelligence Program and culminating two years later with the passage of section 105 of the *Intelligence Authorization Act for Fiscal Year 2002,* the results of numerous meetings, studies, and negotiations ultimately made the Coast Guard Intelligence Program's IC membership possible. However, there was not a straight path to IC membership. Both the HPSCI and CGIP were interested in improving counterdrug and migrant smuggling interdiction efforts. Early on, with the backing of HPSCI Chairman Porter Goss (R-FL), a study of the Coast Guard Intelligence Program (CGIP) was funded, with special attention to be devoted to the question of IC membership.

CGIP staff and the Community Management Staff (CMS) disagreed over the study's report, which did not recommend IC membership. This struggle within the executive branch would shape the debate culminating in the House *Intelligence Authorization Bill for Fiscal Year 2002,* which added the Coast Guard to the list of community members incorporated into the original *National Security Act of 1947.* The heretofore off-the-record initiatives by Intelligence committee staff members, the DCI, Secretary of Transportation, and congressional staff members, revealed here for the first time, reflect a keen power struggle between the Congress and the executive branch.

How Can the HPSCI Help?

The drive toward Coast Guard membership in the Intelligence Community appears to have originated from a briefing on the Coast Guard Intelligence Program in Fall 1998.[127] According to Fred R. "Joe" Call, Coast Guard Office of Intelligence Chief of Staff from 1998 until 2001, the briefing responded to HPSCI

---

127 CGIP is used throughout this publication to refer to the National Foreign Intelligence Element of the Coast Guard. This element was originally incorporated under the Assistant Commandant for Operations and its director was known officially as Chief, Office of Coast Guard Intelligence. In August of 2001 the Chief of the Office of Coast Guard Intelligence position was elevated from GS-15 to a Senior Executive Service position. The new title was the Director of Coast Guard Intelligence.

deputy counsel Chris Barton's request for background on the CGIP. Mr. Barton had visited the Joint Interagency Task Force (JIATF) East in Key West where he received several Coast Guard briefings. He also had visited the Intelligence Coordination Center (ICC), in Suitland, MD.[128] Barton was very interested in counterdrug missions. "He [Chris Barton] wanted to know what resources we needed to do more."[129]

As a member of the HPSCI staff, Barton had a broad perspective of the entire IC not constrained by firewalls[130] or agency stovepipes.[131] The Chief of the Coast Guard Office of Intelligence from 1996 until August of 2001, Dennis Hager, recalled that "Chris Barton was absolutely essential" to the CGIP-IC initiative.[132] Barton was a principal advisor to HPSCI Chairman Goss. Mr. Barton described his job in this way: "I handled the counternarcotics oversight for the HPSCI."[133] Chairman Goss, as a representative from Florida, was very interested in the Coast Guard's counterdrug and migrant interdiction operations.

> My chairman had a long-standing relationship with the Coast Guard. Many of the Coast Guard's missions–Counternarcotics, Counter-smuggling, Alien Migration Interdiction, and Search and Rescue are very relevant to his constituency. People in South Florida are very interested in what is happening with these issues. (If someone sneezes in Havana, Naples and Fort Meyers get colds). Plus, Chairman Goss as a sailor has an appreciation for the maritime mission of the Coast Guard. We were advocates for the Coast Guard.... As the U.S. Navy was moving away from [western] hemispheric missions the CG, despite fewer resources, took on many more training missions which they could have declined. The CG attitude was "How can we do this?" not like some agencies that respond with "We CAN'T do that, we're underfunded, not trained well enough, etc." They were a presence in Panama and had the best information on the Caribbean basin. Chairman Goss was concerned with bringing more and better eyes on these targets. [The] Coast Guard was

---

128 Dennis Hager, former Chief of the Office of Coast Guard Intelligence 1996-2001, interviewed by author 27 May 2003.

129 Commander Fred R. "Joe" Call III, USCG (ret), former Chief of Intelligence Operations, Resources and Planning 1998-2001, and assistant to Mr. Dennis Hager, Chief, Office of Coast Guard Intelligence, interview by the author, 28 April 2003. No formal Chief of Staff position existed, but this best describes his multiple duties as the principal assistant. Mr. Call later became executive assistant to Ms. Frances Fragos Townsend, the first Director of Coast Guard Intelligence. The Office of Coast Guard Intelligence was elevated to Program status in August of 2001.

130 The term firewall as used in the publication refers to the required separation between domestic law enforcement efforts and the collection of National Foreign Intelligence.

131 Mary Sturtevant, "Congressional Oversight of Intelligence," *American Intelligence Journal* 13, no. 3 (Summer 1992):17. Sturtevant was on the professional budget staff of the SSCI, and this article provides great insight into the role and influence of this staff.

132 Hager interview. Nearly every source interviewed referred to Barton as the principal advocate on Capitol Hill.

133 Chris Barton, Deputy Chief Counsel, House Permanent Select Committee on Intelligence, interview by author, 16 June 2003.

the only entity collecting and they needed more money and resources. We needed to help.[134]

Representative Goss' district is in and around Sanibel, on the southern Gulf Coast of Florida. According to Al Bernard, the Coast Guard Liaison Officer to the House of Representatives from 1998-2000, "this was a good issue for him locally. Chairman Goss provided the leadership to get this done."[135] However, prospective CGIP-IC membership impacted far more than Representative Goss' district.

Early Contacts

On 6 January 1999, Dennis Hager and Coast Guard Chief of Operations RADM Ernest Riutta briefed Chris Barton. Admiral Riutta summarized the briefing in an e-mail to the Coast Guard Commandant.

> His [Barton's] primary interest was our intelligence program. Mr. Hager briefed him on our Intelligence Plan and they discussed our possibly moving from GDIP [General Defense Intelligence Program] under ONI [Office of Naval Intelligence] to an intelligence line item of our own under the NFIP [National Foreign Intelligence Program]....He also offered to help us target key Congressmen and staffs to generate support for Use of Force [arming of Coast Guard airborne interdiction assets].... Chris also asked to set up a meeting between you and Congressmen McCollum and Goss to discuss the Coast Guard's role in intelligence. He sees us as a bigger intelligence player in the future, especially in light of Homeland Defense issues that are looming on the horizon and the reluctance of USN and DOD to engage....He clearly is a strong supporter for the Coast Guard, seems very well informed and wants to help us in both Intelligence and counter drug issues.[136]

In an interview, Chris Barton explained his advocacy for the initiative described in this e-mail.

> On a staff level it was my idea for the Coast Guard Intelligence program to enter the IC. It was the right thing [to do] for the country. The Coast Guard is the only agency looking out for our most vulnerable frontier. We were not a committee that traditionally oversees the Coast Guard. There was an evolution of the global threat environment. Based on the nature

---

134 Barton interview.

135 Commander Al J. Bernard, USCG (ret), Coast Guard Liaison Officer to the House of Representatives, 1998-2000, interview by author, 22 April 2003. The author served under Commander Bernard during a previous tour of duty.

136 Rear Admiral Ernest "Ray" Riutta, USCG, Chief of Operations, e-mail to Admiral James Loy, Commandant, Subject "Meeting with Chris Barton, House Permanent Subcommittee[sic] on Intelligence Staff," 13 January 1999. Obtained from Dennis Hager. The HPSCI was not a traditional Coast Guard oversight committee. "Historically the HPSCI had a stretch of a connection with the CGIP." (Barton interview.) The House Transportation and Infrastructure, Coast Guard and Maritime Transportation subcommittee provides primary CG oversight, which might explain the misidentification of the HPSCI as a subcommittee.

of the HPSCI's work we knew about the growing threat of WMD and terrorism. To secure our vulnerable maritime frontier the Coast Guard needed enhanced access to all the Intelligence Community's products.[137]

Barton recalled having asked during a CGIP migration briefing, "How come you [the Coast Guard] haven't gotten all the information on migrant flow?"[138] As a HPSCI staffer, he had access to a variety of intelligence products. As a counterdrug specialist he had observed the success of Coast Guard-run Joint Interagency Task Forces and knew how much the Coast Guard needed access. Barton noted that "over time I have built a tremendous respect for the mission performance of the Coast Guard....My attitude toward the Coast Guard was 'what can we [the HPSCI] do to be helpful? How can we fix the information flow?' We needed to get this done."[139]

Congressman Goss traveled in early 1999 as part of a congressional delegation visiting Haiti and the Dominican Republic and attended a briefing on the Haitian Coast Guard force.[140] In a letter thanking the Commandant for the Coast Guard's support to the delegation, Chairman Goss shared his views.

> Like you, I believe that the Coast Guard is a unique instrument for responding to emerging maritime security issues. As a member of the Aspin Commission, I argued for a thorough reassessment of the Coast Guard's role within the United States national security structure and urged closer coordination between the Coast Guard and the intelligence community. As you develop the Integrated Deepwater System (IDS) to address Coast Guard's acquisition, personnel and operating requirement for the next quarter century, I hope that serious consideration will also be given to incorporating the Coast Guard as a full participant within the National Foreign Intelligence Program....I look forward to meeting with you in the next few weeks on the evolving relationship of the Coast Guard with the intelligence community.[141]

The Coast Guard Intelligence Program (CGIP)

CGIP leadership saw this as an opportunity to fund a comprehensive external evaluation. The focus of the study was not solely on IC membership. The staff hoped the study would help systematically answer Barton's question about the best place to put additional resources.[142] "We were trying to build a brief [reply] back to the HPSCI and recognized that we needed a multiyear plan to digest the funding

---

137 Barton interview.
138 Barton interview.
139 Barton interview.
140 Porter Goss, Congressman, letter to ADM James Loy, Commandant USCG, no subject, dated 5 February 1999 (see Appendix A). Cited hereafter as Goss-Comdt Letter.
141 Goss-Comdt letter.
142 The Coast Guard Intelligence program had received GDIP money since 1990. (United States Coast Guard, "Talking points for G-C (Commandant) / REP Porter Goss (R-FL) 25 February 1999; Hager interview.)

and additional people."[143] Broadening the focus of Coast Guard intelligence was also important because:

> At the time the focus was on counter drug missions... Our mission was to stop smuggling. Not just drugs, but smuggling of all types. We interdict contraband weapons, drugs, money, migrants and potentially WMD [weapons of mass destruction]....be mindful that the Coast Guard Intelligence Program does more than just drugs, the focus can shift fast, as it did on 11 September.[144]

Mr. Call stated that the following four CGIP priorities provided a framework for the future of the program and the external evaluation.

1) Improve CGIP organization and architecture. We [the CGIP] wanted to build a top-down CGIP that managed the program and better served the Coast Guard and National objectives.

2) Exploit technical intelligence advancements and tools.

3) Improve Coast Guard HUMINT.

4) Improve the depth and breadth of our [Coast Guard] analysis.[145]

The CGIP staff was over-tasked and the study provided a way to "contract out for deep thought."[146] Again, the study was not solely to determine whether or not the Coast Guard should be a formal member of the IC. Rather it would provide a growth and implementation plan.[147]

Dennis Hager, Chief of CGIP from 1996 until 2001, saw IC membership as one method to grow the CGIP. The CGIP was constantly competing for resources against new operational equipment expenditures, and repeatedly losing. According to Hager,

> the bottom line for me wanting to take the CGIP into the IC was money, resources. I wanted to build an operational intelligence system that supported Coast Guard operational forces. IC membership was a way to try and get more money for the program from outside the Coast Guard because it wasn't getting enough money from inside the Coast Guard. Generally the trend on the Intelligence budget was flat....We [the Coast Guard] were already going places they [the IC] couldn't go, already doing things they couldn't do, so we were already giving them value. What I was asking for was a bigger share of the pie, based on what we

---

143 Call interview.
144 Call interview.
145 Call interview.
146 Original quote attributed to Captain Stubbs, USCG, who spearheaded the Deepwater program and was referring to the Coast Guard Roles and Missions study. (Call interview.)
147 Hager, Call interviews.

were contributing to that community effort. That was the impetus for CGIP-IC entry.[148]

Talking points written for Admiral Loy described GDIP funding as "invaluable in developing a small but strong intelligence nucleus; however, our intelligence program is under-resourced and is unable to keep pace with our expanding national security missions."[149]

A Unique Opportunity

The political climate from 1998 until 2000 presented a unique opportunity. President Clinton, a Democrat, was in his final two years of office, Republicans controlled the House of Representatives[150] and the Senate was narrowly divided.[151] The Republican-controlled Congress was seeking to gain some victories. House Liaison Officer Al Bernard remembers that "there was a lot of pull [requests for information and sometimes for legislative language] from both the House and Senate."[152] Budgets were shrinking and spending was very tight.

According to the Coast Guard Congressional Liaison Staff, the Coast Guard had two high-priority issues during this period: The Deepwater Project, and Rescue 21. CGIP IC membership was a distant third.[153] The Deepwater Project is a revitalization and recapitalization program that encompasses ships, aircraft, and communications systems under one procurement contract. The Coast Guard and Commandant viewed the combined purchase of these items as crucial to building a truly interoperable command and control system and replacing the aging cutter fleet. Rescue 21 is an upgrade to the nation's maritime distress notification system.[154] To fund these projects, the Coast Guard needed to expand the cap on the Acquisition Construction and Investment portion of the Coast Guard budget from $350 million to $1 billion. Because of these efforts, the Commandant was well

---

148 Hager interview.

149 United States Coast Guard. "Talking points for G-C (Commandant) / REP Porter Goss (R-FL)," 25 February 1999. Obtained from Dennis Hager.

150 The Republicans held 223 seats; 211 seats were held by Democrats and 1 by an independent. *U.S. House of Representatives, Clerk of the House Homepage,* "Congressional History 106th Congress" URL: < http://clerk.house.gov/histHigh/Congressional_History/index.php>, accessed 20 June 2003.

151 The Republicans held 55 seats and the Democrats 45 seats. *U.S. Senate Homepage, Arts and History section,* "Party Division" URL: <http://www.senate.gov/artandhistory/history/common/generic/ party_division.htm>, accessed 20 June 2003.

152 Bernard interview. This direct liaison between CGIP and HPSCI staffs caused internal strife between the Coast Guard congressional affairs and CGIP staffs. Hager and Call interview.

153 Commander Chuck Michel, USCG, Legislative Council, Office of Congressional and Governmental Affairs, interviewed by author 18 April 2003; and Bernard interview.

154 Author's familiarity with these projects comes through numerous briefings and publications presented to Coast Guard Officers. Both initiatives were funded and are ongoing. For more information see the *US Coast Guard Deepwater homepage,* URL: <http://www.uscg.mil/Deepwater/>, accessed 20 June 2003 and *US Coast Guard Rescue21 homepage,* URL: <http://www.uscg.mil/Rescue21/home /index.htm>, accessed 20 June 2003.

known on Capitol Hill. "We did have great relations with the hill. ADM Loy was very responsive to requests for congressional visits and briefings."[155]

In recognition of its priority status and specialized nature, the Coast Guard Liaison Officer to the House of Representatives was content to let the Chief of the Office of Coast Guard Intelligence, Mr. Dennis Hager, "provide the impetus to move [the IC membership initiative] forward."[156] Coast Guard Intelligence and Congressional Liaison staffs had discussed with the HPSCI Staff the proposed external study of the CGIP. The staff inquiries and ties between HPSCI and CGIP burgeoned during the winter of 1999. At one point, Joe Call remembers Chris Barton asking, "Should you guys be a member of the IC?"[157] The staff discussion had percolated up to HPSCI Chairman Porter Goss, who now wanted to meet with the Commandant of the Coast Guard.

A Watershed Meeting

The Coast Guard House Liaison Officer's minutes of the 25 February 1999 meeting between Congressman Porter Goss and Commandant of the Coast Guard Admiral Loy[158] revealed that Chairman Goss was a big advocate of the Coast Guard. The Commandant opened the meeting by stating that "an expanded role in the intelligence community would be a good thing for the Coast Guard."[159] The major concern of the Coast Guard was how to fund the study and secure more resources for the Coast Guard Intelligence Program. The Commandant

> cautioned that he needed a firewall between intelligence money and funds that come into the transportation account. The chairman agreed unequivocally and stated that the Coast Guard continues to be a unique instrument in battling many of the transnational threats facing the nation, including drug interdiction and alien migration.... [Chairman] Goss would like to see an increase in that [GDIP] funding. G-C [Commandant] agreed and stated that a $10-11 million increase would provide more analytical capabilities, which are so important in the current post-cold war era. G-C trumpeted the fact that the taxpayer continues to get the best bang for the buck in all areas, but especially intelligence. Goss agreed and

---

155 Bernard interview. The Commandant needed to be careful when talking on the hill; unlike the Regional Combatant Commanders, he was afforded no immunity and could be held to task for his remarks or testimony by the Secretary of Transportation and other executive branch members senior to him. Based partly on Congress' previous knowledge of Admiral Loy, he was rapidly confirmed as the second director of the Transportation Security Administration in 2002, after his tour as Commandant of the Coast Guard.

156 Bernard Interview.

157 Call interview.

158 Chris Barton, who attended the brief, reviewed and attested to the accuracy of the minutes referenced. Barton interview.

159 Commander A. J. Bernard, USCG Liaison Officer to the House of Representatives, e-mail to distribution, subject "Rep Goss/G-C meeting 2/25/99"(minutes), 26 February 1999. Obtained from Coast Guard Congressional affairs staff, attached as appendix A, cited hereafter as Rep Goss/G-C 2/25/99 meeting minutes.

stated that is why he would like the Coast Guard to be a full participant in the intelligence community...but, he quite frankly stated that he didn't know how to do it...that he would leave to the staffers Chris Barton, Merrill Morehead, and CG to come up with the best solution....Goss told G-C that he knows [the] Coast Guard gets more out of that [GDIP] money than any other agency.[160]

According to the Liaison Officer, the HPSCI "is prepared to be our advocate in securing additional funds in GDIP, but *sees a long term strategy of expanding our role in the intelligence community.*"[161]

The Chairman had granted his support and suggested the Commandant meet with Senator Shelby, (R-AL), chairman of the SSCI, and IC agency heads including Director of Central Intelligence (DCI) George Tenet, to gain support. According to the Coast Guard Liaison to the House of Representatives, "Goss intimated that he would not go forward with any legislation unless the Intel Community is on board."[162] The Liaison officer closed his minutes with a prophetic statement. "It was evident that nothing would be done in FY00, but as the process begins and the committee works with the CG, FY01 or 02 may be target years for legislation to enhance our role in the Intel community."[163] The support was present, now the staffs worked together to devise a strategy and determine how to fund the study.

Staff Work for Funding the Study

Shortly after the meeting between Congressman Goss and Admiral Loy, the CGIP and congressional liaison staffs worked on language for the proposed study.[164] The study funding language was vetted and routed to the concerned offices within Coast Guard Headquarters and then on to the Community Management Staff.

RADM Riutta, Chief of Coast Guard operations, spoke with Tish Long, Deputy Director of ONI, about the study. Ms. Long saw the study as a way to address the Community's concerns regarding Coast Guard membership and get Community buy-in, too. "She is fully behind this approach and feels it is the best way to go."[165] Riutta further characterized his conversation with Long as "totally consistent with

---

160 Rep Goss/G-C 2/25/99 meeting minutes. Congressionally mandating a million dollar study from the Coast Guard's operating expenses would significantly impact the service. The annual operating funds for the USCGC WALNUT, a 225' buoy tender, in FY 03 were $762,215. This excludes a $500,000 supplemental used to outfit the ship for deployment to the Persian Gulf. (E-Mail from LT Rick Boston, USCG District 14 Finance Officer, to author, subject "Operating Expenses for a 225' Buoy tender," 20 May 2003). Funding the study internally could theoretically remove a major Coast Guard Cutter for a year.

161 Rep Goss/G-C 2/25/99 meeting minutes. Emphasis added.

162 Rep Goss/G-C 2/25/99 meeting minutes.

163 Rep Goss/G-C 2/25/99 meeting minutes.

164 Commander Joe Call III, USCG, Chief, Intelligence Planning and Management Division, e-mail to Lieutenant Commander Charles Michel USCG, Legal Office of Coast Guard Legislative Affairs, subject "Proposed Justification for CG Intelligence Program Study," 15 March 1999.

165 Rear Admiral Ernest Riutta, RADM, USCG, e-mail to Commander Fred (Joe) Call, Dennis Hager, and others, subject "RE: Proposed Justification for CG Intelligence Program Study," 16 March 1999. Cited hereafter as Riutta 16 March 1999 e-mail.

Porter Goss' charge to G-C to be sure he lined up the Intel Community behind any effort to change our relationship."[166]

Chris Barton had requested a meeting with Dennis Hager and CMS Staff to

> talk about some "short" legislative language to be included in the upcoming FY00 Intel Auth Bill to provide CG with $$[sic] to conduct a study on the viability of "joining the Intel Community."....Chris states that this is part of a three pronged approach to expanding [the] CG role in [the] Intel community: 1) study; 2) propose findings to the Intel Community; 3) DoD develop I-POM [Intelligence Program Objective Memorandum][167] for expansion of CG role in FY01.[168]

The proposed language was reviewed with the HPSCI staff on Friday, 19 March 1999. This was a unique request. A senior IC source recalled that,

> The CIA's general counsel's office had to research what it meant to be "a named member of the IC." There was no language defining that term or its significance[169]....From the IC perspective the Coast Guard already was a member of the NFIP. They shared space with the ONI at Suitland, they are a GDIP funded intelligence program, they produce intelligence in support of the overall defense intelligence federation.[170]

Briefing the HPSCI Staff, 19 March 1999

Dennis Hager was the principal speaker for the Coast Guard, and Larry Kindsvater, Chief of the Community Management Staff Resource Management Office, spoke for CMS.[171] Together they presented draft language to fund the study of Coast Guard participation in the Intelligence Community. According to the minutes of the liaison officer present,

> the focus of the meeting was to convince the committee to introduce language in the upcoming authorization bill to conduct a study to see if it is feasible to include CG in the Intel community. This study would include

---

166 Riutta 16 March 1999 e-mail.

167 This is a standard method of adding items to the NFIP budget. Dan Elkins, *An Intelligence Resource Manager's Guide,* 6th printing (Washington, DC: Defense Intelligence Agency, 1997), 125. This book provides an excellent overview of the entire Intelligence budget process.

168 Commander A. J. Bernard, USCG Liaison Officer to the House of Representatives, e-mail to Captain Jeffery Hathaway, USCG, and others, Subject "Expansion of CG role in Intl Community – MTG INTEL Subc.[sic]", 15 March 1999.

169 The *National Security Act of 1947* merely lists the members of the Intelligence Community.

170 A source, a senior Intelligence Community professional who wishes to remain anonymous, interview by author, 26 June 2003. Cited hereafter as A senior IC source.

171 Commander Al J. Bernard, USCG Liaison Officer to the House of Representatives, e-mail to Captain Jeffery Hathaway, USCG, and others, subject "Expansion of CG role in Intel Community – HPSCI" (minutes), 19 March 1999. Cited hereafter as CGIP-HPSCI 19 March minutes. Both Hager and Barton attested to the minutes' accuracy. Obtained from Coast Guard Congressional affairs staff.

funding options and recommendations. Hager and Kindsvater provided the staff with proposed language for their review...The [HPSCI] staff was particularly amenable to the study approach and options—Chairman Goss wants a clear and definitive approach to this issue and the study is step one in his approach. Hager also mentioned that the Navy has a marker in the FY-01 I-POM to get started if the study recommends CG involvement.[172]

Hager assessed Kindsvater's actions as playing the field, "He knew Barton and the HPSCI wanted to do this. He has a lot of other CIA things he needs the HPSCI to support...he was trying to stay on the good side of Barton, because later he came out against it [CGIP membership]."[173]

The Coast Guard staff emphasized their desire that Congress fund the study outside of the Coast Guard's typical funding stream and that the current GDIP process be unaffected by the study. The study was expected to cost one million dollars.[174] Barton clearly understood that concern. "In funding the Booz Allen & Hamilton (BAH) [contract] it was important to shield the Coast Guard's normal budget within the Transportation Appropriations bill. Our goal was to do the study with supplemental funding that would not impact the Coast Guard."[175]

In a follow-on e-mail Mr. Hager noted one minor but substantial difference in the language proposed by CMS; *"it did not call for a specific recommendation with regard to membership in the IC."*[176] Barton stated that

> CMS wanted a neutral study with no recommendation for IC membership. I thought it was a waste to spend that much money and not get a recommendation on IC membership. I wanted BAH to use their expertise to make a sound judgment and [employ] research skills to provide a recommendation regarding CGIP-IC membership.[177]

Dennis Hager's opinion was that "CMS intended to conduct the study and have it come out negative,"[178] against the Coast Guard's joining the IC. A senior Intelligence Community source stated "the study was one of many such annual Congressionally directed studies and was funded in the NFIP budget. The study in itself was not controversial."[179]

---

172 CGIP-HPSCI 19 March minutes.
173 Hager interview.
174 Hager, Bernard, Michel interviews; CGIP-HPSCI 19 March minutes.
175 Barton interview.
176 Dennis Hager, Chief Coast Guard Intelligence Program, e-mail to Rear Admiral Ernest Riutta and others, Subject "FW: Expansion of CG role in Intl Community – HPSCI" 22 March 1999. Emphasis added.
177 Barton interview.
178 Hager interview, the subject wanted to emphasize that this was only his opinion.
179 A senior IC source.

A Late Legislative Issue

The legislative session was rapidly coming to a close and funding the study was therefore a late legislative issue. This was significant because "it allowed the language to be put into a bill at conference."[180] According to Commander Bernard,

> Defense was directed to provide 1 million dollars in the Defense Appropriations Bill, which was brilliant because we [the CG] were seriously concerned that the study would be funded from our operating expenses. The funding of the study went through without committee [input]. It was in a conference report in the Appropriations meeting w/ the "Cardinals." He [Goss] already made his deal and used his influence to get the funding for the study into the report language. It was a short order item slid into the bill that was coming to a vote soon.[181]

Barton supplied the language for the House Appropriations Committee, subcommittee on Defense (HAC-D) bill, and the Intelligence Authorization Bill for FY 2000.[182] The HAC-D mark-up language appropriated funds for "a Coast Guard study to be jointly conducted by the Secretary of Defense and the Director of Central Intelligence. The study shall address possible ways in which the Coast Guard can provide additional support to the NFIP."[183] Congressmen Jerry Lewis (R-CA), and Bill Young (R-FL), supported the legislation in the HAC-D.[184] The CGIP had succeeded in funding the study without impacting the traditional Coast Guard operating budget.

According to Barton, "the study was one study among literally hundreds of Congressional[ly] Directed Studies for the DOD and dozens for the IC. It was a one-million dollar item in a DOD budget bill...it was by comparison very small."[185] Approval for funding the study drew little attention.

---

180 Barton interview.

181 Bernard interview, the 13 Chairmen of appropriation subcommittees make up the "cardinals" – the "pope" is the Chairman of the full House Appropriations Committee. Joe Call remembers the funding coming from the *Intelligence Authorization Act for Fiscal Year 2000*. No reference is made to the study in the unclassified sections of this act or the FY2000 Defense Appropriations Acts. The final report was written in response to a combined request of the HPSCI and the HAC. The language funding the study was in the classified portions of these bills.

182 Barton interview.

183 "HAC mark-up language" obtained from Dennis Hager 27 May 2003.

184 Barton interview; Bernard interview.

185 Barton interview.

Initial Reaction to the Concept of IC Membership

The CGIP staff briefed the IC leaders on the study and possible inclusion of the Coast Guard as an IC member. Commander Joe Call was present for many of these meetings. He said that "At the leadership level, Wilson, Jacoby, DIRNSA, DNI thought it was good government. The general consensus from senior IC leadership was that our membership was justifiable and defendable."[186] Ellen McCarthy, who conducted many informational briefings, added that "everyone within the IC thought it was a good idea, so long as it didn't impact his or her resources. The USN and the HPSCI were big backers. Other people gave the proposal a lukewarm reception."[187]

The military people at NSA–Lieutenant General Minihan as DIRNSA, and RADM Windsor Whiteton, head of the Naval Security Group–were supportive. "They saw the Coast Guard as a military service and wanted us to be on board. The uniformed military people welcomed it."[188] Joe Call paraphrased the response of PACOM Director of Intelligence, Rear Admiral Porterfield, to the CGIP brief as "you guys make a good argument for membership but I don't know if I'm going to like it. You'll compete for our resources."[189] This fear of competition for resources was manifested more prominently among the CMS staff, which presented the greatest resistance to CGIP-IC membership.

> The senior IC source interviewed by the author summarized the CMS position as Coast Guard Intelligence Program-IC membership was viewed as a desire to fund the Coast Guard because the Department of Transportation (DOT) was unwilling to fund the needed improvements to the Coast Guard's infrastructure, computers, boats, planes, etc. The IC said it was DOT's responsibility as the parent department of the Coast Guard. It would be equivalent to DIA requesting funds for a new building from the Department of Agriculture rather than from the Department of Defense. I'm exaggerating to make a point.... DOT may not have been the best steward of the Coast Guard, not meeting the basic infrastructure needs of the service and the NFIP was viewed as a funding source.[190]

---

186 Call interview. Hager concurred with this assessment. Vice-Admiral Wilson was the director of DIA, Rear-Admiral Jacoby was the JCS-J2, Lieutenant General Minihan was Director of NSA (DIRNSA) replaced by General Hayden in 1999, and the Director of Naval Intelligence was Admiral Ratcliff.

187 Ellen McCarthy, USCG Office of Intelligence, GDIP budget manager 1998-2001, interview by author. Cited hereafter as McCarthy interview.

188 Hager interview.

189 Call interview. Mr. Call was not sure of the Admiral's exact words and requested it be referred to as a paraphrase.

190 A senior IC source.

The Booz Allen & Hamilton Study

Conceived as a comprehensive year-long examination of the CGIP, the study faced numerous challenges. The late passage of the appropriations bill and complex funding of the study resulted in a significant delay. The funds came from a GDIP account and were transferred from the Department of Defense to the U.S. Navy to the Coast Guard. The Coast Guard then transferred the money to CMS.[191] The contracting process further delayed the study. Finally in June, CMS, with Coast Guard consultation, awarded the contract to conduct a study of the CGIP to Booz Allen & Hamilton (BAH) of McLean, Virginia.[192] One reason given for choosing BAH was the reputation of the proposed study team leader, Vice-Admiral Mike McConnell, USN (ret), former DIRNSA and Joint Chiefs of Staff J2. Hager noted that "I trusted him implicitly to do the study."[193] On 27 June 2000, BAH submitted a program management plan outlining the conduct of the research study. The plan's introduction summarized the genesis and objectives of the study:

> The rapidly changing landscape of U.S. national security objectives and concerns has significantly increased the relevance of traditional and emerging Coast Guard missions. Simultaneously, Coast Guard roles, missions and capabilities provide important opportunities for Coast Guard support to the IC that may justify expanded NFIP support for the Coast Guard. To address potential expanded NFIP support for the Coast Guard, the HPSCI directed an independent study be conducted and reported to the DDCI (CM), GDIP Program Manager, and the intelligence oversight committees. Additionally, the HAC directed a study be jointly conducted by the SECDEF and the DCI to address ways the Coast Guard could provide increased support to the NFIP. This study responds to both Congressionally directed actions.[194]

BAH had six months to gather data and write its report. The study had to be delivered to Congress in January 2001.

BAH Study Team

The Coast Guard contracted Mark Sikorski, recently retired from the Coast Guard, to act as liaison for the BAH study. Sikorski provided the CGIP an inside view of the study, and escorted the BAH study team while it conducted interviews and research.[195] Although VADM Mike McConnell was the BAH study team leader, the project leader was retired U.S. Navy Captain Bill Frentzel, who had served with the Naval Security Group and had cryptological experience.

---

191 Hager interview.
192 Booz Allen & Hamilton, *Coast Guard Intelligence Program (CGIP) Study Program Management Plan* (McLean, VA: Booz Allen &Hamilton, 27 June 2000), 2. Cited hereafter as BAH study management plan; Hager interview.
193 Hager interview.
194 BAH study management plan, 2.
195 Call interview; Mark Sikorski, Coast Guard BAH study liaison officer, Signal Corporation, interview by author 27 May 2003.

Phase I of the study addressed the support the CGIP gave to and received from the IC, and the CGIP-IC relationship. Phase II investigated the current CGIP organization and structure. Phase III provided a functional analysis with recommendations for improved efficiencies.[196] The phase leaders were Cathie Lutter, a specialist on organizational development; Carole Weinraub, human resource management expert; and retired U.S. Navy Captain Roger Messersmith, a joint intelligence, surveillance and reconnaissance expert.[197] According to the study liaison, this team, "as qualified and experienced as they were, had no depth of understanding of the Coast Guard."[198]

A senior steering group (SSG) was also assigned to the study.

A senior level Intelligence Community guidance team is comprised of members from the Community Management Staff, USCG, Office of [the] Secretary of Defense (C3I), DOT (S 60) [Department of Transport, Director, Office of Intelligence and Security], Director of Military Intelligence [Staff, DIA] and the Office of Naval Intelligence. The SSG is a decision-making body and will meet periodically to review contracted deliverables and offer guidance to the BAH Study Team as needed.[199]

Field Research

The Coast Guard tried to help the BAH researchers. The CGIP staff provided a three-page list of interview candidates, IC leaders, Coast Guard partners, and Coast Guard personnel.[200] In a 3 August 2000 message, Rear Admiral Terry Cross, Assistant Commandant for Operations, requested key intelligence commands make all personnel available for interviews, staff visits, and surveys. He ordered each command to assign a CGIP study point of contact. Admiral Cross closed the message by writing, "the short time frame of this important study requires that we devote a significant amount of effort to it if we are to achieve its goals and meet the deadlines imposed."[201]

During August 2000 the BAH team conducted research trips to Coast Guard Headquarters, Coast Guard Intelligence Coordination Center, Coast Guard Groups Key West and San Diego, Coast Guard Law Enforcement Support Group, Coast Guard Atlantic and Pacific Area staffs, and the staffs of the Seventh and Fourteenth Coast Guard Districts. Outside the Coast Guard, the team visited the

---

196 BAH study management plan, 5, 8,9,12,13.

197 BAH study management plan, 17-18; Commandant U.S. Coast Guard, message to Coast Guard Commander Atlantic Area and others, subject, "USCG Intelligence Program (CGIP) Study," 032200Z August 2000. Cited hereafter as CGIP study message; U.S. Coast Guard Headquarters, Office of Intelligence, "US Coast Guard Intelligence Program Study," internal memorandum, 4 August 2000, 2. Obtained from Dennis Hager. Cited hereafter as CGIP study OCI memo.

198 Sikorski interview.

199 CGIP study OCI memo.

200 U.S. Coast Guard, Office of Intelligence, "Listing of Interview Candidates," n.d., obtained from Dennis Hager.

201 CGIP study message. Attached as appendix D.

Joint Interagency Task Forces (JIATF) East and West, U.S. Southern Command (SOUTHCOM), Joint Forces Command, Naval and Marine Corps Intelligence Training Center, Joint Intelligence Center Pacific, and Pacific Fleet Headquarters.[202] One research trip to south Florida illustrated the different viewpoints and capabilities of the Coast Guard and larger intelligence commands at SOUTHCOM and JIATF East.

The team visited the Coast Guard District Seven Headquarters and SOUTHCOM, J2 (intelligence component) in Miami, then the JIATF East and the Coast Guard Group in Key West. The District Commander, Admiral Allen, supported CGIP-IC membership, citing unique access, missions involving transnational issues, and "national security concerns for tomorrow."[203] The intelligence components of JIATF East and SOUTHCOM thought that "the Coast Guard is better off not a IC member...[and should] use the Navy to carry most of the baggage."[204] Sikorski, recalling the trip, said "there wasn't a whole lot of credibility given to the CGIP from the big community side...It seemed like they were focused on [geographically] far away threats. The perception was the Coast Guard was focused on territorial seas and inward."[205]

The contrasting levels of funding and capabilities between Coast Guard and intelligence operations centers was clearly illustrated during the Key West visit. JIATF East is a tactical command focused on drug interdiction in the Caribbean and in waters bordering South America.[206] Group Key West had a much smaller area of responsibility but conducted search and rescue, aids to navigation maintenance, migration interdiction, counterdrug, and other missions.[207] The BAH team was very impressed with the state-of-the-art fusion center and computer technology used at JIATF East. The manual "grease board" tracking of Coast Guard units at Group Key West had the opposite effect.[208] "The JIATF got rave reviews and Group Key West illustrated just how little information the Group was getting and using. This [the contrast in technology and sophistication] left some study members with the impression that the Coast Guard may not be ready to handle IC membership."[209]

Other visits to Coast Guard units and nearby IC facilities left a different impression. Commander Chris Conklin, Chief of Operations and Law Enforcement

---

202 CGIP study OCI memo. No Congressional staff accompanied them during the process, per Sikorski interview.

203 Mark Sikorski, CG liaison to BAH study group, e-mail to Dennis Hager, CGIP chief, and others, subject: "CGD7 Quick Look," 14 August 2000. Cited hereafter as "CGD7 Quick Look."

204 "CGD7 Quick Look."

205 Sikorski interview.

206 *JIATF East homepage.*

207 Author has worked in and is familiar with the Coast Guard Group Key West area of responsibility.

208 "CGD7 Quick Look;" Sikorski interview.

209 Sikorski interview.

for Coast Guard District Fourteen[210] (D14) in Honolulu, Hawaii, summarized the BAH study team visit. "I think they left with a good understanding of what our threats, intel gaps, and needs are…and unique things that the CG could bring to the national intel table from ops in D14 AOR."[211] By early November, the BAH team had competed its data collection and began drafting the final report.[212]

The Draft Report

Mark Sikorski worked to ensure the Coast Guard's concerns were addressed in the report. In a series of e-mails, he discussed the language of the report with project leader Bill Frentzel. The Coast Guard wanted coverage of the IC membership issue and unique statutory authorities of the Coast Guard:

> The IC membership question needs to be prominently discussed in the study, with all of the efforts involved in meeting the CMS requirements, the tight timeline and the obvious politics, that question has lost visibility somewhat. It is very important that the issue is thoroughly explored; please don't misunderstand the CG's position, they don't want to presume membership is in their best interest, but want a rigorous, unbiased examination of the issue.

> The unique statutory authorities of the CG must be in plain view…to lay out the unprecedented opportunities and possibilities that this organization could offer to the IC. Leveraging of its statutory authorities as a military organization and those of a law enforcement agency give the CG a certain amount of "nimbleness" to walk a tightrope that transnational organizations and asymmetric threats are capable of exploiting. [What is required is e]ducating the rest of the IC and Congress that the CG has been walking this tightrope for 10 years already and is well positioned from statutory, organizational and operational perspectives to increase their integration with the IC.[213]

Other e-mails reinforced these themes, addressed specific wording, and countered claims made in the draft report. Sikorski asked BAH to include more "determinant language" in the report and to replace subjective wording. He also suggested a format for the executive summary.[214] He asked them to "tell the CG

---

210 The District Fourteen area of operations (AOR) includes most of the Pacific Ocean south of the Gulf of Alaska, the waters around Hawaii, Guam, and American Samoa. The author was assigned to District Fourteen on board USCGC WALNUT from 2000-2002.

211 Commander Chris Conklin, USCG, Chief of Coast Guard District Fourteen Operations and Law Enforcement Branch, e-mail to Captain Arthur Hanson, USCG, subject "B-A Intel Study Brief," 24 August 2000.

212 Mark Sikorski, CG liaison to BAH study group, e-mail to William Frentzel, BAH study project leader, Subject: "Box Score," 7 November 2000. Cited hereafter as 7 Nov Sikorski e-mail.

213 7 Nov 2000 Sikorski e-mail.

214 Mark Sikorski, CG liaison to BAH study group, e-mail to William Frentzel, BAH study project leader, Subject: "Re: CGIP Study Final Report Outline," 16 November 2000; e-mail from Mark Sikorski, CG liaison to BAH study group, to William Frentzel, BAH study project leader, subject: "Re: Final Report Structure," 19 November 2000.

story. Just as you and your team have grown to appreciate the unique nature of the Coast Guard, I think part of your audience needs to be informed as well."[215] A 22 November 2000 e-mail listed points that the Coast Guard leadership wanted in the final BAH report. These focused the report around answering the question "why the CG?" and included: international organization memberships and access, augmentation of DOD assets, status as lead agency for maritime threats, and ability to "combat transnational threats" as a Law Enforcement Agency, or as an armed service.[216]

The CMS staff and BAH contractor were at odds over classification. BAH attempted to keep the report "For Official Use Only" and had done so with some initial drafts. Toward the end of the study period, CMS informed BAH that the report needed to be classified "SECRET." It was released as, and remains, a classified report.[217]

The Senior Steering Group (SSG)

In late November the SSG met to "review progress and focus on the final report."[218] RADM Underwood, Assistant Secretary of Transportation for Intelligence and Security, and Hager were present. The summary provided for the Commandant discussed the desire to "more clearly show the unique value the Coast Guard would bring to National Intelligence, and specifically answer the congressional question regarding USCG's relationship within the National Foreign Intelligence Program (NFIP)."[219] Some members of the SSG also voiced opposition:

> In a surprising turn of events, during a vigorous discussion of resource implications, the Defense Intelligence Agency (DIA) representative (Ms Kathy Turner) indicated that VADM Wilson [Director, DIA] did not see a value add[ed] for Coast Guard inclusion. This was not consistent with VADM Wilson's previous remarks…While he continues to support USCG as a valuable member of and unique addition to the Intelligence community, he does not support new resources which may come from the General Defense Intelligence Program (GDIP) portion of the National Foreign Intelligence Program (NFIP)….VADM Wilson is supportive, but does not want the costs of a CG program to DIA to exceed the value. We can grow w/o [without] his budget support, but at the end of the

---

215 Mark Sikorski, CG liaison to BAH study group, e-mail to William Frentzel, BAH study project leader, subject: "Re: CGIP Study Final Report Outline," 16 November 2000
216 Mark Sikorski, CG liaison to BAH study group, e-mail to William Frentzel, BAH study project leader, subject: "Additional CG Insight," 22 November 2000.
217 Sikorski interview. The report is available at the Coast Guard Intelligence Intelink homepage.
218 Rear Admiral Terry Cross, USCG Assistant Commandant for Operations, memo to Commandant USCG, subject: "Congressionally Mandated Study of CG Intelligence Program," 11 December 2000. Cited hereafter as 11 December memo. The date is not given. Based on a reference to a briefing the preceding day, the SSG met on 27 November 2000.
219 11 December memo.

day his best chance for getting more $[sic] is to embrace the reality of new threats and organize/prioritize to meet them. We can be part of the solution; challenge is to convince him.[220]

A senior source explained the SSG reaction:

Early drafts of the BAH study report reflected significant Coast Guard Intelligence Program enhancements that required a large infusion of funds. The IC never disputed that, but saw it as a DOT, not an NFIP, problem. Senior executives from around the IC were in unanimous agreement that the Coast Guard was an important contributor to the IC both pre and post 9/11. At issue was who should fund the Coast Guard's modernization of Communications, Computers, Ships, etc. The Coast Guard was lacking fundamental agency infrastructure, namely computer networks and connectivity to operational units. It was about money.

NSA also voiced concerns that the Coast Guard had not informed the Department of Transportation of the IC membership initiative. Subsequently, after a briefing from Director of Coast Guard Intelligence and the Assistant Secretary of Transportation for Intelligence and Security,[221] the Deputy Secretary of Transportation, Mortimer L. Downey, sent a letter of support to Lieutenant General Hayden, DIRNSA.[222] In it he asserts that

this is an opportunity to improve intelligence support to Coast Guard missions, as well as improving foreign intelligence collection capabilities. I support this initiative and look forward to its approval and implementation ...I look forward to increasing cooperation between the Coast Guard and the intelligence community in a world that presents the broadest array of national security threats in our history.[223]

In preparation for a SSG meeting on 21 December, a draft final study report was routed for comment within Coast Guard Headquarters. The Coast Guard drafted a rebuttal of the report's findings, noting that although the Coast Guard "contributes to U.S. national security...Intelligence Community membership is not advised nor necessary for Coast [Guard] Intelligence Program growth."[224] The relations between the CGIP and members of SSG had become strained. Dennis Hager felt that the CMS staff was trying to influence the study's recommendation to be against membership, and fought to counter that. "We fought to the point that I know we were excluded from meetings having to do with the study and the

---

220 11 December memo.
221 Usually a Coast Guard Admiral, this official reports directly to the Secretary of Transportation and is not within the chain of command of the CGIP.
222 11 December memo.
223 Mortimer L. Downey, Deputy Secretary of Transportation, letter to Lieutenant General Michael Hayden, DIRNSA, no subject, 28 November 2000. See Appendix B.
224 Dennis Hager, CGIP director, letter to RADM Terry Cross, USCG Assistant Commandant for Operations, subject: "Coast Guard Intelligence Program Study," 18 December 2000.

contract. They [CMS] didn't want us in the room."[225] The senior IC source recalls, "during the process it [IC membership] was all the Coast Guard reps would talk about, even after 9/11 shifted the focus."[226]

According to Hager, the draft report was full of "non sequiturs."[227] Shut out of the SSG, the Chief of the CGIP sought the advocacy of VADM Mike McConnell, the BAH Study team leader. Mr. Hager said in an interview that McConnell "fought to get it [the study] done and fought for the Coast Guard."[228] The Coast Guard was not even present for the presentation of the final report to CMS.[229]

Reviews of the study assign it a grade from mixed to poor. According to Joe Call, managing the BAH contract was a resource drain. Mark Sikorski, the Coast Guard's liaison to the BAH study team, was kept very busy.[230] "We thought we could overcome the time issue by having BAH use more people, but Lee Carpenter [a Coast Guard Captain] had a great quote. 'If you want a baby it takes one woman nine months. Nine women with one month each won't cut it.'"[231] One staff member assigned to the CGIP said BAH stood for "bad analysis by has-beens."

Mr. Sikorski critiqued the study saying:

> There was a lot of time spent looking at the Coast Guard and Coast Guard mission sets. The intelligence program and how the Coast Guard operated. There was probably less time, or maybe not enough time, spent evaluating its role in the changing world circumstances, because they were changing at the time, to try and put the two together. Not enough time looking at how the program matched emerging threats.[232]

Dennis Hager believes that the study "could have given the Coast Guard a more forceful recommendation for IC membership. But the bottom line is, the report still made the recommendation and it was enough for the Hill to use."[233] The study did recommend and justify Coast Guard membership to the IC.

Impact of Other Studies and Events

The bombing of the USS Cole in Yemen on 12 October 2000 highlighted the importance of Coast Guard capabilities. The U.S. Navy ordered a review of all domestic force protection measures and waterside security measures. "The US Navy has a force projection mission, but the USS Cole bombing illustrated the

---

225 Hager interview.
226 A senior IC source.
227 Hager interview.
228 Hager interview.
229 Sikorski interview; Hager interview; Call interview.
230 CGIP study message; Sikorski interview.
231 Call interview.
232 Sikorski interview.
233 Hager Interview.

need for force protection…. The Coast Guard needed IC membership and greater resources to develop capabilities to help protect Navy assets in homeport."[234] The Commandant in a message to senior commanders delineated "the resources and authorities that can complement existing Navy force protection capabilities."[235] Admiral Loy specifically outlined establishment of restricted areas, security zones, and naval security forces. The port security missions and partnerships with the Defense Department added further merit to CGIP-IC membership.

One other recent study that lent merit to Coast Guard membership was the 1996 HPSCI Staff Study *IC21*. With an entire chapter dedicated to Intelligence and Law Enforcement, the Coast Guard was singled out as the only federal agency that had both responsibilities. Moreover, *IC21* specifically recognized the increasing trend in transnational threats.

> Another factor bringing intelligence and law enforcement together in recent years is that traditional crime issues such as international organized crime, illegal immigration, and money laundering are becoming intelligence topics as they increasingly are viewed by policy makers as threats to U.S. national security.[236]

According to Commander Madsen, Coast Guard Liaison to NSA, "*IC21* saw these transnational issues and asymmetric threats and proposed unique and out-of-the-box-thinking solutions. The Coast Guard fit into that picture. We've been dealing with transnational issues and asymmetric threats for 213 years."[237] Coast Guard admission to the IC could be one way of increasing the Law Enforcement-NFIP interaction advocated by *IC21*.

Although the Coast Guard did not know the outcome of the BAH study, other recent studies had validated the relevance of Coast Guard missions. Among them was the Interagency Task Force on Coast Guard Roles and Missions, which had released its report on 10 February 2000. The report stated that the Coast Guard did have a vital National Security mission in the 21st century.[238] Another was the report of the United States Commission on National Security/21st Century, also known as the Hart-Rudman Report.

The Hart-Rudman Commission, a civilian federal advisory group, was chartered in 1998 by the Secretary of Defense to study U.S. national security and

---

234 Reese Madsen, Commander, USCG Liaison Officer to NSA from 1999-2002, interviewed by author 21 May 2003. Cited hereafter as Madsen interview.

235 Commandant U.S. Coast Guard, message to Coast Guard Commander Pacific Area and others, subject, "Coast Guard Support to navy Domestic Force Protection and Waterside Security Requirements," 182118 January 2001.

236 U.S. Congress, House of Representatives, Permanent Select Committee on Intelligence Staff Study, *IC21: Intelligence Community in the 21st Century,* 104th Congress (Washington, DC: GPO. 1996), 272-273.

237 Madsen interview.

238 Joint Interagency Task Force on Coast Guard Roles and Missions, "Report of the Joint Interagency Task Force on Coast Guard Roles and Missions." URL:<http://www.uscg.mil/news/reportsandbudget/rolesandmissions/R&M.html >, updated 10 February 2000. Accessed 16 May 2003.

develop a strategy to meet the emerging threats of the twenty-first century.[239] Its reports and research predated 11 September 2001 and coincided with the CGIP-IC entry process.

The first phase of this report, released 15 September 1999, addressed the expected world situation in the next 25 years, and accurately predicted the attacks by terrorist groups on American soil. It went on to suggest a "blurring of boundaries between homeland defense and foreign policy."[240] The second phase of the report, released 15 April 2000, designed a national security strategy to fit the expected world situation presented in phase one. This strategy called for the Department of Transportation to be more fully integrated into the national security process and listed "*homeland security* [sic] capabilities" as one of five fundamental military capabilities.[241]

Phase three of the report proposed specific changes to the national security structure to implement the strategy proposed in the previous report, and was released on 15 February 2001. "Securing the National Homeland" was one focus of the report, which recommended the creation of a National Homeland Security Agency that would include the Coast Guard. The report emphasized the critical border security and prevention role of the Coast Guard. It also called for "bolstering the intelligence gathering, data management, and information-sharing capabilities of border control agencies to improve their ability to target high-risk goods and people for interdiction."[242]

One other Congressionally-directed study supported IC membership for the Coast Guard. Section 308 of the *Coast Guard Authorization Act of 1998* had directed the Secretary of Transportation to "establish a task force to assess the adequacy of the Nation's marine transport system."[243] The report, submitted to

---

239 *The National Security Study Group Homepage*, "About us, Charter," URL: <http://www. nssg.gov/About_Us/Charter/charter.htm>, accessed 23 June 2003.

240 The United States Commission on National Security/21st Century, "New World Coming: American Security and the 21st Century, Major Themes and Implications, the Phase I Report on the Emerging Global Security Environment for the First Quarter of the 21st Century" *The National Security Study Group Homepage*, "Reports," URL: <http://www.nssg.gov/reports/NWC.pdf>, accessed 23 June 2003, 3, 4, 7,8.

241 The United States Commission on National Security/21st Century, "Seeking a National Strategy: A Concert for Preserving Security and Promoting Freedom, the Phase II Report on a U.S. National Security Strategy for the 21st Century" *The National Security Study Group Homepage*, "Reports," URL: <http://www.nssg.gov/phaseI1.pdf>, accessed 23 June 2003, 14.

242 The United States Commission on National Security/21st Century, "Road Map for National Security: Imperative for Change, the Phase III Report on the U.S. Commission on National Security/21st Century" *The National Security Study Group Homepage*, "Reports," URL: <http://www. nssg.gov/phaseIII.pdf>, accessed 23 June 2003, viii,12, 13.

243 *Coast Guard Authorization Act of 1998*, Public Law 105-383, Section 308. 13 November 1998.

Congress in 1999, demonstrated the strategic and economic value of U.S. ports.[244] It identified "increasing national security needs" as a critical issue facing the Marine Transport System (MTS). It also pointed out the need for, but continuing prohibitions on, the sharing of "intelligence information related to security threats and vulnerabilities" within port facilities.[245]

The bombing of the USS *Cole* dramatically increased the U.S. Navy's concern about domestic Naval base security. The internal roles and missions study of the Coast Guard reemphasized the relevancy and need for a strong and capable Coast Guard. *IC21* discussed the need for overlapping intelligence and law enforcement operations. The Hart-Rudman Report addressed the pending threats facing America and highlighted an increased homeland security and intelligence role for the Coast Guard. And finally, the MTS report to Congress highlighted the importance of, and need to protect, U.S. ports. All these reports combined with the BAH study to bolster the case for CGIP-IC entry.

BAH Study Findings and Endorsements

Delivery of the Study's Report to CMS

The CGIP was in position to exploit the study's recommendations. Dennis Hager summarized the BAH report for the Chief of Legislative Affairs by writing that the study,

> looks favorable for USCG in most respects except recommend appropriations process (DOT). Believe HPSCI will find it to their liking and work with us to fix that problem. Have learned that Rep Goss would like to look at some draft legislation to implement study recommendations before he comes over for working lunch so that he and G-C [Commandant] can discuss.[246]

Although the CGIP was the subject, BAH conducted the study for CMS and Congress. The DDCI (CM) was principal recipient of the report, and that office did not agree with all the recommendations. "CMS has already chosen to disinvite us to the final report brief. (We believe because the support staff decided before

244 Waterborne cargo adds over $742 billion to the U.S. gross domestic product; 90 percent of all equipment and supplies for Operation Desert Storm were shipped from U.S. ports. U.S. Department of Transportation, *An Assessment of the U.S. Marine Transportation System, Report to Congress,* September 1999, URL: <http:www.dot.gov/mts/report/>, accessed 23 June 2003. Cited hereafter as *MTS Report to Congress.*

245 *MTS Report to Congress.*

246 Dennis Hager, Chief CGIP, e-mail to Captain Robert Papp, USCG, Chief, Congressional and Governmental Affairs Staff, subject "Intel Study Update," 9 February 2001.

the study was even started that they would not endorse any resource increases for Coast Guard and they do not want any dissension.)"[247]

Regardless of CMS reactions, HPSCI staffer Barton agreed with the recommendation for the CGIP to join the IC.

> The Booz Allen & Hamilton [BAH] study provided factual basis for an idea whose time had not only come but was long overdue....The Coast Guard needed access, and without membership the IC was not going to provide or share intelligence. The agency charged with defending our vulnerable yet vital maritime frontier needed to be part of the NFIP team....Had Booz Allen & Hamilton said IC entry was a bad idea, it would not have gone forward.[248]

CMS Reaction

BAH delivered the final report of the study on 8 February 2001.[249] The report did not receive a ringing endorsement by all parties. Kevin Powers from the NSA's Office of the General Counsel expressed a concern that a Coast Guard boarding officer, conducting law enforcement operations predicated on intelligence, could be subpoenaed to testify in subsequent legal proceedings.[250] Such testimony could compromise intelligence-gathering sources and methods.[251] The NSA legal staff "was absolutely adamant that the Coast Guard, as a law enforcement agency, could not join the IC."[252] A major CMS concern was that IC membership would be a resource drain rather than a funding source for the Coast Guard: "The study showed many areas where the Coast Guard could benefit from additional funding. It illustrated the impact more money would have on Coast Guard intelligence production."[253] Joe Call recalled that the CMS staff feared

> that the increased oversight and IC membership overhead (joint committees, reports, budget resource proposals) were ultimately going to hurt us [the Coast Guard]. It could in fact offset, erode or diminish the benefits of joining the IC. To remain compliant with all the requirements would require a negative gain on our resources.[254]

---

247 Dennis Hager, Chief CGIP, e-mail to Lieutenant Commander Donald Jaccard, USCG Congressional and Governmental Affairs Staff, and others, subject: "RE: Intel Study Review," 15 February 2001. Cited hereafter as Hager-Jaccard 15 Feb e-mail. Hager confirmed this assertion in the 27 May 2003 interview.

248 Barton interview.

249 Talking points are internal memoranda used for senior personnel during meetings and phone calls, and direct quotation would not reflect what was said. The points listed do represent the agenda intended by subordinates and theoretically the leadership. U.S. Coast Guard, Office of Intelligence, talking points, "G-C Meeting with Representative Goss," 15 March 2001. Cited hereafter 2001 G-C/Rep Goss talking points.

250 Michel, Hager interviews. The author received no response from telephone messages and e-mails requesting an interview from Kevin Powers, NSA Office of the General Counsel.

251 Michel interview.

252 Hager interview.

253 A senior IC source.

254 Call interview.

According to Hager, "CMS fought it because prior to 9/11 intelligence budgets were shrinking and they knew that any money we [the Coast Guard] were going to get would be coming out of somebody else's pocket."[255]

> CMS, as the first recipient, put their endorsement on the BAH report before sending it to Congress. This endorsement would be the subject of negotiations that reached cabinet level. There was a consensus to forward [the] study to [the] Hill with [a] cover letter that the community would have to take a further look at the study to "validate" findings....This could be construed as stonewalling and [I] would expect that Hill staffers would not be pleased.[256]

Commander Madsen, Coast Guard Liaison Officer to NSA, described the reaction there as "binary, people either thought it was a great idea or were not in favor of it. There was little middle ground. Most NSA people that were opposed (to CGIP-IC entry) did not fully appreciate how the Coast Guard operates and our use of intelligence."[257] CMS had not objected to the idea of the study, but they didn't foresee the results.[258] In response to the negative reaction the report received from CMS, Dennis Hager wrote in an e-mail to a Coast Guard staffer:

> This does not surprise us as we have known all along that the Intelligence Community will not give us anything that might take away from their own legacy budgets despite the changing world dynamics and new emerging threats to our nation. *That is in fact why this is [a] congressionally directed as opposed to intelligence community effort–and why it is so important for us to weigh directly into the congressional process.*[259]

Coast Guard Response

The CGIP staff was not responsible for congressional liaison nor for writing draft legislation. This placed the Chief of Intelligence in a precarious position, necessarily responding to HPSCI inquiries while trying to maintain the established internal Coast Guard bureaucratic liaison chain. One thing that allowed him to circumvent the normal routing and response chain was the unique nature of the HPSCI and IC in general. The Coast Guard Congressional and Governmental Affairs Staff did not have the clearances and program knowledge needed to respond to HPSCI inquiries. The CGIP staff was performing a balancing act between abiding by established Coast Guard Congressional Liaison protocols and promptly responding to HPSCI oversight and inquiries. According to Commander

---

255 Hager interview.
256 Dennis Hager, CGIP Chief, e-mail to Rear Admiral Terry Cross, USCG and others, subject "FW: First Word On Coast Guard Study Brief To CMS," 27 February 2001. Cited hereafter as Hager-Cross "first word" e-mail.
257 Madsen interview.
258 Bernard interview.
259 Hager-Jaccard 15 Feb e-mail. Emphasis added.

Call, the relationship between the CGIP and Coast Guard Congressional Affairs "was bumpy at times."[260]

Hager and the CGIP staffers knew they had a limited window of opportunity. The recommendations of the BAH study would lose luster after a year or two.[261] Determined to push CGIP–IC membership, Hager responded to the Congressional Affairs staff concerns by writing we must "be very careful not to put bureaucratic process sensitivities before principle. Go slow on this and it will fail from bureaucratic inertia."[262] Al Bernard agreed and stated that for Hager IC membership was a priority and that "this would have taken years had we gone through the traditional process."[263]

There were other internal fears that the CGIP had burned bridges within the IC, but Hager allayed these fears:

> There are sensitivities in the community, particularly on the money manager's side where any initiative that is not theirs is considered a turf raid. This is not a new thing and after the fight is over everybody generally gets back together....[M]uch of the top leadership are far more open-minded and understand the value added we are proposing and are in fact supportive of us.[264]

Hager pushed forward with the initiative and began to address IC concerns. In an attempt to counter the negative endorsement from CMS, a separate Department of Transportation endorsement of the study was proposed. The CGIP began working within its Department to garner support.[265]

With study and recommendation in hand, HPSCI staffer Barton requested another meeting between Chairman Goss and Commandant Loy.

Second Meeting between Chairman Goss and Admiral Loy

In e-mails about preparing Admiral Loy for the second meeting, Commander Steve Poulin wrote that the recommendation for CGIP-IC membership was correctly based on Coast Guard locations and missions. Additionally, he identified Chairman Goss as our champion in the House. "Rep. Goss may prove to be our champion on the Hill and can hopefully overcome any reluctance that could surface from the intel community, appropriators, or other cognizant authorizing committees."[266] Commander Poulin recognized that no corresponding Senator had

---

260 Call interview.
261 Sikorski and Hager interviews.
262 Hager-Jaccard 15 Feb e-mail.
263 Bernard interview.
264 Hager-Jaccard 15 Feb e-mail.
265 Hager-Cross "First Word" e-mail.
266 Commander Steve Poulin, CG Congressional and Governmental Affairs, e-mail to Mark Sikorski, USCG, subject "RE:Intel Study One Page Brief" 23 February 2001. Cited hereafter as Poulin 23 February e-mail.

yet to emerge and that the political viability the initiative may have held outside the HPSCI was uncertain.[267]

Admiral Loy met once again with Chairman Goss on 22 March 2001.[268] The briefing notes prepared by the CGIP staff express support for CGIP entry into the IC. They state that "attaining community membership is *good government*– it supports Coast Guard operations and national security objectives…Under any definition, I expect the Coast Guard to have an important role in national security."[269] Addressing the primary reason for opposition, the notes recognized the good working relationship in place between the IC and the CGIP. No minutes exist of the meeting but, according to Barton, the meeting "reaffirmed support." [270] Barton recalls that "Admiral Loy never advocated the plan. He was not opposed as long as it didn't hamper the traditional Coast Guard budget."[271] The Commandant as a leader in the executive branch could not come out in favor of something that was not in the President's budget or lacked his support.

Internal Department of Transportation (DOT) Briefings

CGIP briefed the Coast Guard Chief of Operations, who briefed the Commandant, who briefed the Secretary of Transportation, Norman Mineta.[272] Within DOT, RADM Jim Underwood (USCG), the Director, Office of Intelligence and Security (S-60), sent a memorandum to Secretary Mineta on 28 March 2001 summarizing what transpired at the 27 March meeting with CMS.

> Yesterday I attended a meeting with key players of the Intelligence Community Management Staff (CMS) who have drafted the NFIC's response to the Hill regarding the study. Their key point was the study does not make a compelling case to bring the Coast Guard into the NFIC. The Coast Guard agrees that the study fails to adequately address the changing emphasis of national security towards homeland security and asymmetric threats that are clearly areas where Coast Guard intelligence currently provides and could increasingly provide invaluable information in the future. I anticipate Admiral Loy will be providing you with additional information about the various issues of concern regarding NFIC

---

267 Poulin 23 February e-mail.

268 The previous liaison officer had left and the Office of Congressional Affairs had changed leadership. After a thorough and exhaustive search of electronic archives, no record of the 22 March 2001 meeting between Porter Goss and the Commandant was discovered. Given the sensitivity of closed-door meetings on the Hill and new leadership, the author suspects the distribution of these minutes had been severely curtailed and controlled.

269 2001 G-C/Rep Goss talking points. This does not reflect what was said at the meeting but rather what was written to prepare the Commandant for the meeting. Italics and underlining in original.

270 Barton interview.

271 Barton interview.

272 Secretary Mineta had served as a U.S. Army intelligence officer and correspondingly had a good understanding of intelligence. *U.S. Department of Transportation homepage*, "U.S. Transportation Secretary Norman Y. Mineta" URL: < http://www.dot.gov/affairs/mineta.htm>, accessed 23 June 2003.

membership, potentially seeking your approval to pursue membership notwithstanding the CMS response as well as seeking your endorsement to a Coast Guard letter to the Hill concerning the study findings.[273]

Secretary Mineta wrote his endorsement the same day. "Let's move forward on trying to stop CMS letter to the Hill and get me an appointment with Adm Loy to meet w/ [sic] Mitch Daniels [Director of OMB]."[274]

Admiral Loy formally requested "approval to pursue making the Coast Guard part of the National Foreign Intelligence Community"[275] in a memorandum to Secretary Mineta on 29 March. He also requested the Secretary's "assistance in gaining approval by outside agencies and Congress."[276] Admiral Loy summarized the CMS staff objections to membership, noting that "the community feels that there will be no funding growth in the National Foreign Intelligence Program (NFIP) to fund Coast Guard national intelligence collection and analysis, reducing the available funds for current member agencies."[277]

The Commandant provided his recommendation

to pursue membership without funding now and develop a firm funding strategy with concurrence from your staff. I understand from your comment to RADM Underwood that you may favor Coast Guard funding as a fifth armed service within the General Defense Intelligence Program (GDIP).[278]

Admiral Loy requested that Secretary Mineta help the CGIP-IC entry effort "through your contact with the Director of Central Intelligence and other cabinet-level officials."[279] The Commandant closed the letter by offering his assistance in the meeting with Mitch Daniels and preparing an Administration response.[280]

273 Admiral Jim Underwood, USCG, DOT S-60, memorandum to Secretary of Transportation Norman Y. Mineta, subject: "Coast Guard Inclusion in the National Foreign Intelligence Community," 28 March 2001. Cited hereafter as S-60-SEC DOT memo.

274 S-60-SEC DOT memo.

275 Admiral James Loy, USCG Commandant, memorandum to Secretary of Transportation Norman Y. Mineta, subject: "Coast Guard Wants to Join the National Foreign Intelligence Community," 29 March 2001. Cited hereafter as COMDT-SECDOT 29 March memo.

276 COMDT-SECDOT 29 March memo.

277 COMDT-SECDOT 29 March memo.

278 COMDT-SECDOT 29 March memo.

279 COMDT-SECDOT 29 March memo.

280 COMDT-SECDOT 29 March memo.

With the talking points, the Coast Guard was attempting to blunt the negative cover letter to be submitted with the study on 31 March 2001.[281] The Coast Guard senior leadership all agreed that CGIP-IC membership was needed and important. Everyone from the Secretary of Transportation to the CGIP Chief agreed with the BAH study recommendation for IC membership. Based on talking points given to Secretary Mineta for a 29 March 2001 conversation with the Deputy Director of Central Intelligence for Community Management Affairs, Ms. Joan Dempsey (DDCI-CM), the Secretary supported CGIP-IC membership. The talking points referred to the Coast Guard's law enforcement and military roles, unique access to international organizations, and geographical range. As a final point, it documented Secretary Mineta's preference to present one view from the administration.[282]

In an interview, the Chief of the CGIP during this time, Dennis Hager, summarized the results of these efforts, saying "we succeeded in getting the CMS letter rewritten. The initial recommendation was totally negative. The final endorsement was not positive, but it was a lot more positive than before."[283]

CMS Endorsement

The CMS endorsement to Congress was drafted with a request for additional study. According to a senior IC source,

> In the IC/DoD letter forwarding the study to the Congress, we acknowledged that Coast Guard intelligence does good work but we did not support the implication that the next dollar the NFIP spends should go to the Coast Guard because there are many competing priorities. It would be as if the DIA had contracted a study to see how much DIA production would increase/improve with more money. With more funding DIA could do this. It allows DIA to approach the DCI and say I have a report that says DIA is swell, it could do much more with more funding. What is to dispute? Any organization should be able to make that claim. What was in dispute was where to put the next dollar, what to fund. We sensed that the purpose of the study was to get the Coast Guard more money, and the Coast Guard even said so.[284]

The fight over the study's endorsement was over.

---

281   The documents referred to are: "Talking points for G-O (Assistant Commandant for Operations, Admiral Underwood). RE: Membership in the National Foreign Intelligence Community" 26 March 2001; "Talking points for G-O RE: CMS Response to Coast Guard Intelligence Security/ MDA (Maritime Domain Awareness)" 27 March 2001; "Talking points for G-O RE: Relationship of Intelligence Study to Homeland Defense/Security/MDA," 26 March 2001; "Talking points for G-C (Commandant) G-C Phonecon with Secretary Mineta," 28 March 2001. Obtained from Commander Michel, USCG.
282   "S-1 talking points for Director OMB: On Coast Guard Intelligence Program Study," 29 March 2001. Ms. Dempsey was incorrectly identified as Director OMB vice Director CMS. This is indicative of how little DOT or CG staff worked with CMS.
283   Hager interview.
284   A senior IC source.

Despite the prospect of CMS' negative endorsement, on 30 April 2001 Chris Barton asked for draft legislative language adding the CGIP to the IC.[285] The language was included in the HPSCI version of the Intelligence Authorization Bill for FY2002. It was not included in the SSCI version of the bill. The CGIP and Chris Barton had yet to find a champion in the Senate.

Actions to Strengthen Support

In the summer of 2001 the CGIP began implementing some of the BAH study recommendations. The position of Director of the Office of Intelligence was elevated to a Senior Executive Service position from a GS-15 position in August of 2001 and Frances Townsend was assigned as Director of Coast Guard Intelligence.[286] Coast Guard liaison officers and members of the CGIP staff began briefing members of the IC about Coast Guard intelligence. Mark Sikorski remembers "Ellen McCarthy and I probably put together fifteen to twenty briefs.... those briefings started in March 2001 and extended into the summer."[287] The liaison officer to NSA recalls:

> My mission was to educate other NFIC members about the Coast Guard. I took every opportunity to market the Coast Guard. I would speak at seminars, sit on panels and answer questions. [In] nine out of ten events, the audiences during the briefing and after were very interested in the CGIP-IC membership. Most were interested in what we brought to the community and how we could develop our capabilities. How we would fit in and operational differences from the Navy and other IC members. The audiences just did not understand the Coast Guard's capabilities and missions nor did they have many opportunities within the IC to be exposed to the Coast Guard and our missions.[288]

The principal staff supporter on the Hill, Chris Barton, was busy as well:

> I would arrange to have other staffers visit the ICC and Coast Guard HQ to try and learn more about the Coast Guard and CGIP. What I was trying to do was build a consensus and support for the Coast Guard's ongoing missions in support of the war on drugs. Congress does oversight and part of that oversight can be advocacy.[289]

On 30 April 2001, Barton helped organize a trip to the ICC in Suitland, Maryland. Nineteen staff members from both Houses and numerous committees

---

285 Dennis Hager, CGIP Chief, e-mail to Capt Ahern, USCG, and others, subject: "Draft Intel legislation request," 30 April 2001.
286 Hager, Call interviews:
287 Sikorski interview.
288 Madsen interview.
289 Barton interview.

went along.[290] On Friday, 18 May 2001, Barton hosted a CGIP briefing for interested congressional staffers.[291] His invitation to other staffers said the briefing would provide a summary of current CGIP activities, the findings of the BAH study, USCG response to the study, need and justifications for NFIP membership, resource requirements associated with the initiative, and legal authorities needed to accomplish the initiative.[292] Because only two staff members had clearances, Majority Staff director Rebecca Dye requested a separate unclassified CGIP briefing for the staff of the Coast Guard and Maritime Transportation Subcommittee.[293] One other reason for the separate briefing Barton mentioned was that the staffers "were reluctant to go [to briefings] and were surprised that the HPSCI had any jurisdiction over the Coast Guard."[294]

A Power Shift in the Senate

Senator Jeffords (I-VT) announced on 24 May 2001 that he would become an independent and caucus with the Democrats, providing them a majority of one and transferring power in the Senate from the Republicans to the Democrats.[295] Effective 6 June 2001, control of the Senate shifted, along with chairmanship of all the committees. The SSCI chairman had been Senator Shelby (R-AL). Senator Graham (D-FL) now took over as Chairman of the SSCI.[296] An article in *Roll Call* called the relations between committees after the switch excellent. "Goss called it 'just a bit of serendipity' that the Senate Intelligence panel is now helmed by his 'personal friend' and fellow Floridian Sen. Bob Graham."[297]

According to the Chief of the Office of Congressional Affairs, Admiral Robert Papp, Jr., "The biggest senatorial advocate [for Coast Guard IC membership] was Senator Bob Graham of Florida.... Senator Graham was, in general, a great

---

290 Lieutenant Commander Donald Jaccard, USCG Office of Congressional Affairs, e-mail to Ellen McCarthy, CGIP, subject: "RE: Hill Staffer Briefings," 23 April 2001. Staff from the Armed Services, Appropriations, and Intelligence committees, along with one from the Senate Committee on Commerce, Science and Transportation, and two personal staff members attended.

291 Commander Karl Schultz, USCG Congressional Liaison Officer to the House of Representatives, email to Mr Dennis Hager, Chief, CGIP, subject "CG & MT Subcommittee Briefing on the CG Intel Program: Request for Weds 5/30 @ 1300" 21 May 2001. Cited hereafter as Schultz-Hager 21 May e-mail.

292 Schultz-Hager 21 May e-mail.

293 Schultz-Hager 21 May e-mail. They were staff members of a subcommittee of the House Transportation and Infrastructure Committee; Barton interview.

294 Barton interview.

295 *U.S. Senate Homepage,* "Art & History , senators who switch parties" link, URL: <http://www.senate.gov/artandhistory/history/common/briefing/senators_changed_parties.htm>, accessed 2 July 2003. In the House of Representatives, the Republicans held 221 seats and maintained control, 212 seats were held by Democrats and 2 by independents. *U.S. House of Representatives, Clerk of the House Homepage,* "Congressional History, party divisions" URL: <http://clerk.house.gov/histHigh/Congressional _History/partyDiv.php>, accessed 7 July 2003.

296 Rear Admiral Robert Papp, Jr., Chief, Coast Guard Office of Congressional Affairs, 1999-2002, interview by author 23 June 2003. Admiral Papp was a Captain during this time period. Cited hereafter as Papp interview.

297 Ben Pershing, "Goss on a Mission," *Roll Call,* 4 October 2001. According to the article, then-Governor Graham appointed Goss to the Lee County Commission, starting his political career.

Coast Guard supporter."[298] Admiral Papp said this support was based largely on Bob Fillipone, a Graham staffer who was very favorably impressed by the Coast Guard.[299]

All these efforts would be augmented by the Coast Guard's response to the terrorist attacks of 11 September.

Tragic Catalyst

Porter Goss introduced House Resolution 2883, the Intelligence Authorization Bill for Fiscal Year 2002, which became Public Law 107-108, on 13 September 2001, just two days after the tragic attacks of 11 September. The shrinking resources of the IC were about to change drastically as money flowed into intelligence budgets. Asymmetric threats against our nation had been devastatingly manifested by the attacks on the World Trade Center and Pentagon. According to most CGIP staffers, the attacks of 11 September eroded all opposition. Commander Michel said, "Absent 9/11 I don't know whether it would have passed. The timing was critical."[300] Joe Call asserted that "without the catalyst of 9/11, the CMS staff was in a position to stop CG-IC membership."[301]

Chris Barton stated that,

[i]n the pre 9/11 environment these resource mangers were still looking at a "Zero-sum game". This was not in the president's budget nor was it a DCI initiative. Post 9/11 the Coast Guard had proved itself particularly in NYC where they secured the port and directed the evacuation by sea of lower Manhattan. There was recognition of the need and performance.[302]

With the additional money and the effectiveness of the terrorist attacks, CMS opposition to Coast Guard IC membership faded. House Report number 107-219 justified Coast Guard inclusion. It read:

The Commandant of the Coast Guard recently explained that the definition of national security "has widened to include many of the things for which the Coast Guard has been responsible for years. The so-called asymmetric array of threats are now added to the classical inventory of nation-state engagement, potentially leading to armed conflict. It certainly now includes counter-terrorism, counter-narcotics, illegal alien smuggling and worrying about our Exclusive Economic Zone." The Coast Guard is

---

298 Papp interview.
299 Papp interview.
300 Michel interview.
301 Call interview.
302 Barton interview.

the only organization responsible for law enforcement, intelligence and military activities simultaneously.[303]

House resolution 2883 passed the House by voice vote on 5 October 2001.

H. R. 2883 was received by the Senate, the language of Senate resolution 1428 was substituted, and the bill passed by voice vote on 8 November 2001.[304] One of the differences between the House and Senate versions was Section 105, "Codification of the Coast Guard as an element of the Intelligence Community." The bill was going to conference.

The Fight Before Conference

If the scuffle between CMS and the CGIP over language in the report was heated, the fight to influence the conference between the HPSCI and SSCI members grew in horsepower and intensity. The Coast Guard drafted a letter from the Secretary of Transportation to Chairman Goss in support of the Coast Guard entry. In it the Secretary expressed "my strong support for your committee's intention to establish the U. S. Coast Guard as an element within the Intelligence Community....I believe this act is especially warranted given the recent terrorist attacks."[305] The letter places the Secretary clearly in favor of IC entry.

E-mail correspondence provides further information about the origins and history of this draft letter.

> CG [wrote] a letter from the Secretary to Goss, as Goss requested, to support the language naming CG as an agency in the National Foreign Intelligence Program. The House Intelligence bill passed before we could get the letter up. Then we tried to get it up for the record; Jane DeCell said OMB had to clear it. OMB said No because they were going to do a SAP [Statement of Administrative Policy]. Then we found out they were not going to do a SAP and the Committee [HPSCI] really wanted the letter. Today [26 October 2001], OMB finally cleared the letter; then a minute later, Michael Cassidy called me back to say that he saw an old DCI comment on this issue in the bill. *Their [CMS] objection is apparently not to CG being named, but to the legislative issue. The President has the power to name any agencies* [as IC members] *he wishes—DCI was concerned about this precedent usurping the President's power.* If it was

---

303 H. Rept. 107-219.

304 *Thomas legislative information on the Internet homepage*, Library of Congress, 107th Congress Public Laws, "107-108," link, Bill Summary & Status section. URL: < http://thomas.loc. gov/bss/d107/d107laws.html>, accessed 25 June 2003.

305 Norman Y. Mineta, Secretary of Transportation, DRAFT letter to Honorable Porter Goss, HPSCI Chairman, no subject line, no date. See Appendix C. Cited hereafter as DRAFT SEC DOT-HPSCI letter.

deemed necessary by the President, he could do it himself. So, no on the letter again![306]

The Coast Guard was in a precarious position. Engaging Congress on the issue of membership was only possible if there was no SAP against membership.[307] Admiral Harvey Johnson directed the Chief of the Office of Coast Guard Congressional Affairs

> to continue to engage with the Senate....If OMB decides to issue a SAP opposing the legislation, then that avenue is closed and we are almost back to square one. Kathleen [DOT staff] then opens the door to working the issue from inside the Administration. Something we know will be a very difficult sell. In fact, *it is the difficulty of the issue inside the Administration and Intel community that sparked the legislative initiative.*[308]

Senate Supporters

Congressional Affairs staff worked in the Senate to inform staffers of the benefits of CGIP-IC membership. Captain Papp talked with Deputy Majority Staff Director of the SSCI, Bob Fillipone.[309] Papp explained in an interview, "Bob Fillipone was interested in intelligence and interested in supporting the Coast Guard."[310] Fillipone had worked with the Coast Guard on the Port Security Commission and transferred from Senator Graham's personal staff to the SSCI.[311]

> Bob was well aware of the language in the House Bill and indicated that he has had conversations already with Chris Barton. Bob's opinion was that it made great sense to include the CG as a named member, particularly since the events of 9/11...He was inclined to support the House language in conference, but wanted to know where the Commandant stood on

---

306 Kathleen Kraninger, Office of the Secretary of Transportation, e-mail to Manson Brown and others, subject: "Chairman Goss letter and Intel Bill," 25 October 2001. Italics added.

307 Statements of Administrative Policy (SAPs) are definitive. Publicly renouncing one would be equivalent to defying the President.

308 Rear Admiral Harvey Johnson, USCG Office of Operations and Capabilities, e-mail to Captain Robert Papp, USCG Chief of the Office of Congressional Affairs, and others, subject: "RE: Chairmen Goss letter and Intel Bill," 26 October 2001.

309 Papp, promoted to rear admiral in 2002, had met Fillipone at a Coast Guard Congressional Affairs education event known as "Coast Guard Missions Day." Designed to raise awareness of Congressional and Administration staff, the event includes a C-130 flight to Coast Guard Training Center, Yorktown, VA. Displays and activities are set up to highlight Coast Guard missions, including Coast Guard cutter tours, Law Enforcement shooting simulators, small boat piloting, and displays of environmental clean-up actions. Both Admiral Papp and Commander Bernard credit this program with increasing CG awareness on the Hill and gaining supporters. Up to 60 staffers could attend each event and they started in 1999. Bernard and Papp interviews.

310 Papp interview.

311 Captain Robert Papp, USCG, Chief of the Office of Congressional Affairs, e-mail to Rear Admiral Lower Half Harvey Johnson and others, subject: "RE: Chairman Goss letter and Intel Bill," 26 October 2001. Cited hereafter as Papp-Johnson e-mail.

the issue. I told him the Commandant strongly supported the House efforts...[312]

The Coast Guard had found a powerful staff advocate in the Senate—the principal intelligence advisor to SSCI Chairman Bob Graham. According to the Chief of the Office of Congressional Affairs, "Senator Graham in particular was interested in the Coast Guard and saw us as an agency to be admired, one that did our job well and was very professional."[313]

Chris Barton in an interview concurred, stating that:

> Bob Fillipone, who worked on Maritime issues for Senator Graham, was another supporter and assigned to the SSCI staff. Senator Graham was also an ally of the CG and directed a study on Maritime threat [*An Assessment of the U.S. Marine Transportation System*, a report to Congress in September 1999] coincidentally with the Booz Allen Hamilton [BAH] study. Both were major works that supported our initiative for Coast Guard Intelligence Program (CGIP) entry into the IC.[314]

Commander Chuck Michel, the Coast Guard legal advisor for this initiative, listed five benefits of having the membership designation in legislation:

(1) every other member is included by statute;

(2) legislation makes membership more permanent and not subject to executive whim;

(3) legislation gets the CG name in front of Congress and the intelligence committees;

(4) after 9/11 CG missions, performance and need for intelligence are high profile;

(5) given prior CMS objections/concerns, legislation avoids what could very well be a losing [interagency] fight for the CG.[315]

While the advocates for membership were clear, the opponents were also presenting the case against membership.

Senate Opposition

Although the CGIP-IC initiative had the solid backing of both the HPSCI and SSCI chairmen, it had garnered at least one potential opponent. The staff

---

312 Papp-Johnson e-mail.
313 Papp interview.
314 Barton interview.
315 Commander Charles Michel, USCG Office of Maritime and International Law, e-mail to Captain Robert Papp, USCG Office of Congressional Affairs, and others, subject: "RE: Chairman Goss letter and Intel Bill," 26 October 2001; Michel interview.

for Senator Shelby, former Chairman of the SSCI and the Transportation Appropriations Subcommittee before the power shift, was believed to be opposed to the Coast Guard's joining the IC.[316] Admiral Papp explained:

> I don't personally have any recollection of Senator Shelby speaking out against it [CGIP-IC membership]....His appropriations staff was opposed to our full membership. I think for relatively altruistic reasons they saw it as being; here's the Coast Guard complaining about not having enough money to do operations,[317] yet they want to branch out into something that will likely cost even more money. So as appropriators, they are reluctant to sign off on something that is going to cost them more money and perhaps cut back on Coast Guard operations in other areas, unless we get fully funded for it. That was their primary concern....I think the appropriators saw it as: here we are complaining about too many missions and not having enough money to do the missions we have already and we're trying to branch out into another mission area.[318]

As the ranking member of the Transportation Appropriations Subcommittee that approved the Coast Guard's budget, Senator Shelby was not an adversary the Coast Guard could afford to have. Barton recalled that

> Senator Shelby was harder to read on this. Senator Shelby could influence the Transportation Appropriations. Bill [Duhnkle][319] and Captain Papp of the Coast Guard Congressional Affairs staff were concerned about potential repercussions of going against Senator Shelby. I don't think Senator Shelby felt that strongly. This was resolved at the staff level. Congress responds to the mail and this was generating no mail [constituent interest].[320]

Richard Best, National Security specialist at the Congressional Research Service, noted that he received no inquiries from Congressional staff of members before the bill went to conference.[321]

Community Management Staff

In a letter to Chairman Porter Goss, DCI Tenet spoke out against CGIP inclusion:

> I am concerned with House language that would place portions of the Coast Guard within the Intelligence Community. I believe this action is

---

316 Michel, Papp, Barton interviews.
317 A fifteen-percent reduction in operations had been proposed; only supplemental funding bills passed after 9/11 allowed the Coast Guard to restore operations. (Papp interview).
318 Papp interview.
319 SSCI minority staff director from June 2001-2002.
320 Barton interview.
321 Richard Best, National Security Specialist, Congressional Research Service, interview by author 23 April 2003. Best wrote a memorandum on the impact of IC membership to Coast Guard missions in April 2002.

premature given the events of 11 September and the stand-up of the new Office of Homeland Security. The proposal should be reviewed more thoroughly and I request the conferees rescind the House language.[322]

Although the language expressed the DCI's objection, it was not a strong rebuke of CGIP-IC membership.[323]

The CIA circulated a draft conference letter stating its position on the *Intelligence Authorization Act for Fiscal Year 2002*. The draft conference letter clearly stated CIA's opposition to Section 105 of House Resolution 2883 and also any alternative avenues for the CGIP to pursue membership:

> The Administration believes the case for taking such action has not been made and that it would be premature to proceed with this idea. There could be adverse consequences if sections 101(12) and 105 become law without the opportunity for the Administration to address fully the funding, authorities, and other practical issues that placing a law enforcement agency in the IC would raise. The administration notes that section 3(4)(J) of the National Security Act of 1947 (50 U.S.C.401a(4)(J))[sic], already authorizes the President acting alone, or the Director of Central Intelligence (DCI) and Secretary of Transportation acting jointly, to designate the Coast Guard or components of the Coast Guard as elements of the IC.[324]

A senior IC source described the letter from CMS as appealing against the initiative despite the BAH study recommendation and support of both chairmen. The source explained that "appeals are part of the process. Even though both chairmen may favor a section, that doesn't mean the executive branch will not voice their opposition. It just makes overturning or removing that language less likely."[325] CMS and the DCI were weighing in against Section 105, and opposing both SSCI and HPSCI Chairmen.

CGIP Supporting Information in Response to the CMS Letter

With the DCI opposed, the CGIP and CMS staff worked to influence language and argue their position. The main CGIP point was that the Coast Guard as a military service should join the IC. The CGIP argued the Coast Guard's broad statutory authority, extensive experience in countering asymmetric operations,

---

322 George J. Tenet, Director of Central Intelligence, letter to Honorable Porter Goss, HPSCI Chairman, no subject listed, date stamped "HPSCI 11/07/01, 043107 PM." Note: the author received only page five of this letter, which contained both the text and signature. Source: Dennis Hager.

323 "One man's premature is another man's forward leaning." Papp interview.

324 Central Intelligence Agency, "Conference letter on H.R. 2883," no date but fax transmission indicates 20 November 2001. This letter is stamped "DRAFT." The author found no official SAP on record, but this may have been an "advance copy" to inform the committees about CIA views without formalizing the correspondence. Similarly, the only copy of the letter from Secretary Mineta was also marked "DRAFT."

325 A senior IC source.

international access, and worldwide maritime expertise, all validated by the BAH study, were justification for IC membership. The Coast Guard Intelligence Program realities refuted any claims that this was a resource grab, because for every dollar of NFIP money, the CGIP invests four and one half dollars from internal funds.[326] Lastly the Coast Guard argued that its missions are not presently represented at senior-level sessions: "without advocacy, some CG/maritime priorities never see daylight."[327]

The resource argument is hard to refute and illuminates a common question in the IC: How does one assign value to intelligence work? A senior IC source stated the problem in this way:

> For forty years the IC has been trying to determine what is the quantifiable value of intelligence? What is one intelligence report worth? Based on intelligence spending, what is returned to the taxpayer? It is not like a business. In a manufacturing business, you know how much you spend on material and production, and based on that you price your product to sell at a profit. Intelligence products are very difficult to quantify. I am unaware of any metric for gauging productivity or usefulness. If the Coast Guard has one, I'm sure Director Tenet would love to use it. I want to emphasize that I appreciate Coast Guard intelligence; whether it is a bargain or rip off? I don't know.[328]

No objective measure of the value of intelligence products can be applied universally throughout the Community. Coast Guard-supplied intelligence that is of great value to a maritime analyst may be of no value for a weapons systems analyst. Without an objective universal metric the value of intelligence remains dependent on the user's needs and hard to quantify.

CMS Rebuttal to the CGIP Supporting Information

The CMS rebuttal to the Coast Guard's supporting information drew attention to the potential loss of unique information collection access due to association with the IC, and to "the risks of subjecting sources and methods to the law enforcement process [which] requires careful scrutiny."[329] CMS expressed concerns that the BAH study focused on potential benefits of IC membership but did not address the relative value of current contributions, and

> the contractor's conclusions left too many unanswered questions about funding, ...legal implications, and ultimately what benefits would accrue to the IC....Unless the Coast Guard budget is taken out of Transportation altogether, and taken out of the jurisdiction of the DoT's authorizers and appropriators, it is not clear what benefits will accrue. This points out

---

326 "USCG response to CMS draft," notes from Dennis Hager, no date.
327 "USCG response to CMS draft," notes from Dennis Hager, no date.
328 A senior IC source.
329 "CMS rebuttal to Coast Guard response," no date (fax transmission lists 3 December 2001). Provided by Dennis Hager. Cited hereafter as "CMS rebuttal."

the need for further refinement of the proposal following more careful review.[330]

Frances Townsend

In August of 2001 the Coast Guard selected Frances Fragos Townsend, former deputy to U.S. Attorney General Janet Reno from 1995 to 1998 and head of the Justice Department's Office of Intelligence Policy and Review, as its first Director of Intelligence.[331] According to Ellen McCarthy, Ms. Townsend was well-known in the Community and had lots of contacts. When she arrived "she was told to make IC membership happen and did so."[332]

As the bill was approaching conference, the new Director of USCG Intelligence met with staffers of the HPSCI, SSCI, CMS, and the office of the DCI. Through her contacts, she could gauge reactions to letters and endorsements. "Barton was not terribly worried about the DCI letter….he has spoken with the SSCI staff and believes that they will not be swayed by the DCI letter. Barton indicated that Sen Graham is also a believer in this effort."[333]

Ms. Townsend reviewed the DCI's language and stated that "we need to get SSCI's sense of the impact of the DCI letter on our effort. The language in the DCI letter is not favorable but could have been much worse."[334] She discussed the language with colleagues at CIA, setting up a meeting on Friday 9 November.

> I indicated to CIA that I was surprised by the language in the DCI's letter [such as] "premature" and needed to be "reviewed more thoroughly" given the $1 million Booz-Allen report for which CIA/CMS let the contract. My sense thus from CIA is that their objection to our membership in the community is not a substantive one, rather they believe that our only interest is financial. I really believe that the USCG's commitment to the program in our current budget should help to convince them otherwise.[335]

She met with CIA staff on 9 November 2001.

---

330 CMS Rebuttal.

331 Frances Townsend, PBS frontline interview transcript, "The Man Who Knew," interviewed 30 May 2002. URL: <http://www.pbs.org/wgbh/pages/frontline/shows/knew/interviews/townsend.html>, accessed 27 June 2003; McCarthy interview.

332 McCarthy interview. Ms. McCarthy agreed with the author's birth analogy for the CGIP-IC process. If Dennis Hager and Chris Barton where there from the conception of this initiative, Frances Townsend was the midwife called in to deliver the breech-baby of CGIP-IC membership.

333 Frances Townsend, Director of CGIP from 2001-2003, e-mail to ADM Timothy Josiah, USCG Chief of Staff, and others, subject: "FW: FY-03 Homeland Security Re-Rack," 7 November 2001. Cited hereafter as Townsend 7 Nov e-mail.

334 Townsend 7 Nov e-mail.

335 Townsend 7 Nov e-mail.

In notes from the meeting, she explains the nature of their objections to CGIP-IC membership and how these were countered:

> CMS staff and management are not supportive of our effort to get community membership although they softened when I explained that this was not simply a ploy on our part to get NFIP funds, rather a sincere attempt to improve our ability to serve national interests by: increased coordination, increased access by USCG and the intelligence community to each others' information and the intelligence community's ability to provide both tasking and oversight of intelligence activities. I also pointed out that mere membership has no downside for the community. If they don't believe the program deserving they need not provide additional funds and membership does not of right entitle USCG to "a seat at the table" in terms of resource allocation. CMS staff found the conversation reassuring as they did not believe that this had been clearly understood. They asked several questions that indicated that they did not understand what benefit there would be to the community for USCG to be a member....Our greatest advocate at CIA is Charlie Allen, Assistant Director of CIA for Production & Analysis....[I]t was worth making the point to CIA that if we are currently providing intelligence on national requirements why should they not acknowledge that by agreeing to membership which would also provide greater operational efficiency to USCG by focusing our security efforts with the increased access to intelligence that this would mean. In the end, the staff seemed more open although not enthusiastic about USCG. My assessment and several at CIA agreed was that with a call from S-1 to DCI, the DCI might agree to membership or to stand aside quietly while the Bill goes to conference and see what happens....CIA seemed genuinely surprised that USCG was still interested and pushing membership....However, they were very honest that the CIA position up to now was determined at a mid-manager level and had not ever been briefed to the DCI so no one knows what he will think.[336]

Thanks to Ms. Townsend's contacts, the Coast Guard knew better just how strongly opposed CMS was to the bill and why.

Additionally, Director Townsend further gauged activities in the Congress by calling the primary Coast Guard advocate for this measure, HPSCI deputy general counsel Chris Barton. Ms. Townsend expressed her concern over the strength of support for the measure in the SSCI "given that at least two SSCI staffers are former CIA attorneys. Chris agreed that they [the SSCI] are not as strong as [in the] HPSCI but believes that USCG will prevail because this is important to

---

336 Frances Townsend, Director CGIP 2001-2003, e-mail to Admiral Timothy Josiah, USCG Chief of Staff, and others, subject: "Update re: CIA," 12 November 2001. Cited hereafter as Townsend 12 Nov e-mail.

Goss and Graham."[337] Townsend advocated direct contact between Secretary of Transportation Norman Mineta and DCI Tenet to persuade Tenet to endorse the measure.[338]

The 29 November 2001 American Bar Association conference on National Security Law provided an excellent opportunity for the new CGIP Director to work on the CGIP-IC membership initiative.[339] Townsend had lunch with SSCI General Counsel Vicki Duvoll and two other SSCI staff members. Ms. Duvoll said that the SSCI staff had been working to garner CIA support for CGIP-IC entry. The SSCI general counsel asserted "that it is now clear that the USCG provision is going to be in the final language after conference regardless of CIA's position because the members are committed to it."[340] At the same meeting, CIA CMS staff approached Ms. Townsend about planning for implementation after passage of the measure.[341] A briefing for the SSCI staff was planned for 3 December 2001.

The 3 December 2001 SSCI staff briefing allowed the Coast Guard to make a case for IC membership just prior to the bill's going to conference.[342] One SSCI staffer requested bullets that discussed the initiative. For the final time before conference, the CGIP again made its familiar argument for membership. The bullets highlighted the Coast Guard's status as an armed force, its unique capabilities, and the recommendation of the BAH study. It refuted Community opposition to membership based on perceptions that the initiative was a resource raid by noting the small percentage of NFIP funds that the Coast Guard receives and by highlighting the ratio of internal CGIP funding to the amount of NFIP funding, roughly 4.5 to 1.[343] The bullets concluded that the Coast Guard needs access to Community information, membership validates the Coast Guard's existing intelligence contributions, and the IC would benefit from a maritime perspective and Coast Guard effort against smuggling.[344]

---

337 Townsend 12 Nov e-mail.

338 Townsend 12 Nov e-mail.

339 Frances Townsend e-mail to Admiral Timothy Josiah, USCG Chief of Staff, and others, subject: "Re: FW: LRM MGG169 - - Central Intelligence Agency Conference Document on HR28...," 29 November 2001. Cited hereafter as Townsend 29 Nov e-mail. Townsend is a lawyer.

340 Townsend 29 Nov e-mail.

341 Townsend 29 Nov e-mail.

342 The previous liaison officer had left and the Office of Congressional Affairs had changed leadership. After an exhaustive search of electronic archives, no record could be found of the 3 December SSCI briefing or 22 March 2001 meeting between Porter Goss and the Commandant. Given the sensitivity of closed-door meetings on the Hill and new leadership, the distribution of these minutes may have been severely curtailed and controlled.

343 U.S. Coast Guard, Office of Intelligence, "Coast Guard Membership in the Intelligence Community, Main Points," 4 December 2001. Attached to Ellen McCarthy, CGIP, e-mail to CAPT Robert Papp, USCG Office of Congressional Affairs and others, for distribution to Jim Hensler, Deputy Minority Staff Director for the SSCI, subject: "SSCI Request for Bullets–Time Sensitive," 4 December 2001. See Appendix D. Cited hereafter as CGIP SSCI bullets.

344 CGIP SSCI bullets.

Conference

The Intelligence Authorization Bill for Fiscal Year 2002 went to conference with both chairmen in favor of the provision in Section 105 adding the Coast Guard to the list of IC members, but with the staff for the SSCI vice chairman and the executive branch opposed. What actually happened in the committee meeting is unknown. No public record was provided or kept. A committee report was written and sent to both the House and Senate. The only insight into this conference might be from staff members who were present. When asked during an interview about the controversy generated by Section 105, Chris Barton replied, "At the staff level there was protest by a member of Senator Shelby's staff, but that was just as the FY 2002 Intelligence Authorization Bill was going to conference [5 December 2001]. Prior to that this was low profile."[345]

Going into conference, the Chief of the Office of Coast Guard Congressional Affairs, Admiral Papp,

> was convinced that we were going to fail on the Senate side and I really think it was a force of personality. This is just my opinion, I think Fillipone convinced Senator Graham that he, as Chairman, was just going to have to say unilaterally that this is the way it was going to be, because I know Shelby was objecting. I never heard Shelby directly but that was characterized in reports to me.[346]

Barton in an interview later stated simply, "Senator Graham did the push-back in conference. This was not a hard sell based on Coast Guard performance [response] during 11 September."[347]

Regardless of what transpired in conference, on 6 December 2001 the conference report, House Report 107-328, was filed. This report summarized the conference action on codification of the Coast Guard as an element of the IC by simply stating, "Section 105 is identical to section 105 of the House bill. The Senate amendment has no similar provision. The Senate recedes."[348] The President signed the bill into law on 28 December 2001.[349] On that day, with the passage of the *Intelligence Authorization Act for Fiscal Year 2002*, the Coast Guard Intelligence Program became part of the National Foreign Intelligence Community, as designated in the *National Security Act of 1947*, as amended.

---

345 Barton interview.
346 Papp interview.
347 Barton interview.
348 U. S. Congress, House of Representatives, *Intelligence Authorization Act for Fiscal Year 2002, Conference Report*, 107th Cong., 1st session, 6 December 2001, H.Rept. 107-328, 1, 18.
349 Public Law 107-108, *Intelligence Authorization Act for Fiscal Year 2002*. (28 December 2001).

Initial Impact of Membership

A senior IC source interviewed by the author saw little impact to the IC from inclusion of the Coast Guard:

> This is a case study of "what's in a name?" So now the Coast Guard is a "named member," so what? What's changed? From my perspective this was a misguided effort from the start. What has changed? Two seals were put on the wall, one in CIA headquarters and one in the HPSCI conference room. The internal changes, elevating the Intelligence program to an Assistant Commandant position, was a very good move, but could have been done by the Coast Guard. In terms of GDIP funding and missions, little has changed. The CG intelligence budget grew after 9/11, just as the other IC budgets grew after 9/11. If I were to ask an intelligence analyst in the Coast Guard prior to IC membership, are you a member of the Intelligence Community? They would have answered yes, based on their job and mission. After IC membership I would get the same answer. Based on funding and missions the Coast Guard already was an IC member. This initiative was a pursuit of more funding.[350]

This statement reflects the views of one person inside the Community. The perspective from outside the named Community differed.

> For the Coast Guard membership had a more pronounced affect. Chris Barton recalled a conversation about the impact of membership with the director of Coast Guard Intelligence, Frances Townsend. She described the Coast Guard's situation prior to 9/11 as standing outside two big glass doors looking into the IC. The day after the President signed the bill into law the doors were opened and the CGIP had access. This access substantially contributed to the CGIP's ability to work.[351]

Mark Sikorski believed IC membership added legitimacy to the Coast Guard Intelligence Program and facilitated information sharing. He elaborated on the need for membership:

> It opens other doors for the Coast Guard to expand its capabilities. If you read the tea leaves there is a very real possibility that some component of the next terrorist attack will have a maritime nexus to it. I think that it enables the CG now to expand and become an even more professional intelligence program.[352]

True to Dennis Hager's prediction, no bridges were burned in the IC membership process. Barton described relations this way: "[A]s soon as the President signed the bill the relationship with the CMS staff turned around 180

---

350 A senior IC source.
351 Barton interview.
352 Sikorski interview.

degrees, and a good relationship with ONI got better."[353] According to a Senior IC source, after membership, the CGIP was still too small to construct its own budget or resource proposals. The CGIP lacked the funding to pay for services or space that had been utilized before IC membership at no cost.[354] "The Intelligence Community generally agreed to continue providing the Coast Guard with all of those services and facilities at no cost."[355]

Joe Call, executive assistant to the Director or the Coast Guard Intelligence Program, explained relations between the IC and CGIP since inclusion:

> Joan Dempsey [DDCI-CM] has been very impressed with all we've gotten done to date. She even told Ms. Townsend that she is impressed with the amount of work her staff has finished based on its small size. We are not a pariah or black sheep. Everyone knows what we contribute and 9/11 sharpened our mission profile and increased IC resources.[356]

Ellen McCarthy described the progress made by the Coast Guard Intelligence Staff and the unique attributes that continue to make the Coast Guard a valued IC member:

> We are moving along and are already far ahead of some IC agencies with our relationships to local law enforcement agencies and the maritime industry. The CMS staff since our entry has been very helpful and pleased. They have directed us to seek out new ways to do things in hopes of discovering a better way or process. There is a hope that the Coast Guard can become the model for some of the ongoing issues.[357]

Despite the opposing views on IC entry, since the passage of Section 105 of the *Intelligence Authorization Act of 2002,* support from the CMS has been outstanding. In the words of a senior IC source, "[t]he entire IC wants Coast Guard to succeed."[358]

---

353 Barton interview.

354 Rent for ICC space shared at ONI facilities, and education funds and staffing demands for schools such as the Joint Military Intelligence College and Joint Military Intelligence Training Center are some examples. JMIC asked for a Coast Guard instructor on staff in 2002, and the funding received from the NFIP may be subject to a "Community tax." Previously received CGIP funds were shielded from such "taxes."

355 A senior IC source.

356 Call interview.

357 McCarthy interview. Relations between local law enforcement and industry are one example. The Coast Guard Marine Safety Program has a long-standing cooperative relationship with port and maritime professionals. Coast Guard law enforcement operations work with multiple agencies.

358 A senior IC source.

CONGRESS LEADS REFORM OF THE INTELLIGENCE COMMUNITY

> This was one of the best things I've done in government service.
>
> — *Chris Barton, HPSCI General Counsel*

Oversight or Management

The entry of the Coast Guard Intelligence Program into the Intelligence Community represents a milestone in Congressional oversight of the IC. It represents the first time that the Congress has added a new member against the recommendation of the DCI. It sets a legislative marker in the "operationalization" of the Intelligence Community concept by setting a precedent for future modification of IC membership through legislation.

Chronological Summary of the CGIP IC entry

Congress has been directly involved in adding the last two members of the Intelligence Community: the intelligence elements of the Coast Guard and Department of Homeland Security.[359] In the late 1990s, Congress also directed the creation of NIMA after eliciting a promise to do so from DCI Deutch at his confirmation hearing. Several factors contributed to the realization of CGIP entry into the IC. From initial brainstorming by one HPSCI staff member to IC membership required countless hours of effort, a one million-dollar study, and endless wrangling and negotiations among bureaucrats. Such intensive behind-the-scenes maneuvering is apparently not unusual.

The initiative started in spring 1999 with an agreement among the HPSCI, CMS, and CGIP to fund a study assessing the merits of IC membership for the Coast Guard Intelligence Program. HPSCI Chairman Porter Goss added language funding the study to the *Intelligence Authorization Act for Fiscal Year 2000* when the bill was in conference. Chris Barton, HPSCI General Counsel, also provided language which Representative Bill Young (R-FL) added in conference to the corresponding *Defense Appropriations Bill for Fiscal Year 2000.* The Community Management Staff (CMS) awarded the contract for the study to Booz Allen & Hamilton (BAH), which conducted the CGIP study in the fall of 2000. Prior to

---

359 The executive branch appears to have "struck back" in the contest for naming new members of the Community with the early 2006 addition of the Drug Enforcement Administration as a component member. This addition apparently came about as a combined executive action by the Director of National Intelligence and the U.S. Attorney General. See http://www.fas.org/irp/news/2006/02/odni021706.html.

---

issuing a final report, both CMS and the CGIP attempted to influence the report's recommendation for CGIP IC membership. BAH submitted the report to CMS on 8 February 2001 with a recommendation for CGIP inclusion. A disagreement, reaching as high as the Secretary of Transportation and Deputy Director of Central Intelligence for Community Management (DDCI-CM), ensued over the wording of CMS' forwarding endorsement letter to Congress. Congress received the BAH report recommending CGIP IC entry with a contrary endorsement from CMS on 31 March 2001.

Chris Barton and CGIP gained support for the entry initiative by educating Congressional staff members. The bombing of the USS Cole and the 11 September 2001 terrorist attacks highlighted the importance of Coast Guard missions and the need for greater intelligence access. The HPSCI included a provision in the House version of the *Intelligence Authorization Bill for Fiscal Year 2002,* which amended the *National Security Act of 1947* by adding the CGIP to the IC members listed in Section 3(4)(H) of the Act. The Senate's version of the bill did not contain this provision. Both bills passed their respective chambers and went to conference. CMS and CGIP staff presented opposing viewpoints on the CGIP IC membership provision to the Senate Select Committee on Intelligence. The measure survived conference and the President signed the *Intelligence Authorization Act for Fiscal Year 2002* on 28 December 2002, making it law.

Figure 4 depicts chronologically the actions of the Coast Guard Intelligence Program Staff, CMS, and Congress that contributed to CGIP IC membership. "External events" that potentially influenced the process are highlighted in the figure.

DATE	Coast Guard Actions	CMS Actions	Congressional Actions
Pre-1999	Tours of intelligence facilities		Chris Barton works counterdrug issues
6 January 1999	Brief for Barton		Attended intel brief
January 1999			Rep Goss (R-FL) visits Haiti
25 February 1999	Meeting w/Rep Goss		Meeting w/CG Commandant

Continued on next page

DATE	Coast Guard Actions	CMS Actions	Congressional Actions
26 February 18 March 1999	Work on study funding language	Reviewed study funding language	
19 March 1999	Meeting among CGIP, CMS, and HPSCI Staff to discuss funding and nature of CGIP study		
15 September 1999	Hart-Rudman Phase I report describing global threats for next 25 years released, highlighting increased homeland security role		
September 1999	U.S. Maritime Systems report submitted to Congress identifying increasing need for intelligence information to secure ports		
6-8 October 1999			CGIP Study funding put in Defense Appropriations bill at conference by Rep. Young (R-CA).
25 October 1999			FY 2000 Defense Appropriations bill signed into law
9 November 1999			CGIP Study funding put in FY 2000 Intelligence Authorization bill at conference by Rep. Goss (R-FL)
3 December 1999			FY 2000 Intelligence Authorization Act signed into law

Continued on next page

DATE	Coast Guard Actions	CMS Actions	Congressional Actions
2000			
15 April 2000	Hart-Rudman Phase II report designed a national security strategy, which included homeland security as one of five fundamental capabilities and highlighted increased DOT role		
Spring 2000	Awarded contract to Booz Allen & Hamilton (BAH) to conduct CGIP Study		
27 June 2000	Hired Mark Sikorski to assist BAH study team	CGIP Study plan received from BAH	
August 2000	BAH field research at Coast Guard facilities, JIATFs, Combatant Commands		
12 October 2000	USS Cole bombed in Yemen. Domestic port security concerns raised by the U.S. Navy. Coast Guard capabilities critiqued.		
November 2000	Work began on draft BAH report; Sikorski works to include CGIP issues into report		
27 November 2000	CMS voiced opposition to CGIP-IC membership at Senior Steering Group		
28 November 2000	Assistant Secretary of Transportation wrote to DIRNSA supporting CGIP IC entry		
21 December 2000	BAH report draft circulated to CMS CGIP for comments		

Continued on next page

DATE	Coast Guard Actions	CMS Actions	Congressional Actions
2001			
8 February 2001	CGIP received report, but was not invited to final BAH CMS briefing	BAH final report submitted to CMS, recommending CGIP-IC entry	
15 February 2001	Hart-Rudman Phase III report released recommending IC changes to bolster intelligence capabilities of border control agencies		
22 March 2001	Meeting w/Rep Goss		Meeting w/CG COMDT
27 March 2001	CMS draft endorsement against IC membership for CGIP reviewed; representative from DOT present		
28 March 2001	Secretary of Transportation (SECDOT) favors IC membership		
28-31 March 2001	Negotiations between SECDOT and CMS softened negative endorsement language		
28-31 March 2001	Negotiations between SECDOT and CMS softened negative endorsement language		
31 March 2001	CMS endorsement and BAH study delivered to HPSCI and SSCI		
April-August 2001	CGIP staff briefed IC audiences about CGIP capabilities and contributions		
30 April 2001	Hosted 19 Congressional Staff for ICC tour		Barton helped organize ICC tour and requested IC entry language

Continued on next page

DATE	Coast Guard Actions	CMS Actions	Congressional Actions
18 May 2001	Conducted CGIP brief on the Hill for Transportation Subcommittee staff		Barton hosted CGIP subcommittee briefing for staff
6 June 2001			Sen. Jeffords (I-VT) broke away from the Republican party. Democrats take control of the Senate. Sen. Graham (D-FL) replaced Sen. Shelby (R-AL) as SSCI Chairman.
August 2001	SES hired as Director of CGIP		
11 September 2001	Terrorists attacked World Trade Center and Pentagon.		
13 September 2001			Goss introduced FY 2002 Intel Authorization bill in House, w/provision for CGIP IC entry
14 September 2001			Graham introduced Senate version of FY 2002 Intel Authorization bill lacking CGIP IC entry provision
5 October 2001			Bill passed House
8 November 2001			Bill passed Senate

Continued on next page

DATE	Coast Guard Actions	CMS Actions	Congressio- nal Actions
October 2001	Letter drafted by SECDOT supporting IC membership		
7 November 2001		DCI Tenet calls CGIP IC membership premature in letter to Rep. Goss	
9 November 2001	CGIP Director (Townsend) met with CIA Staff advocating CGIP IC membership		
20 November 2001		Draft "conference letter" faxed to HP- SCI opposes CGIP IC entry	
29 November 2001	CGIP Director (Townsend) met with SSCI Staff members at American Bar Association conference on "Intelligence and the Law." SSCI Staff expressed support for CGIP entry. CMS attorneys asked about CGIP integration plan for entering the IC.		

Continued on next page

DATE	Coast Guard Actions	CMS Actions	Congressional Actions
3 December 2001	CGIP Staff briefed SSCI Staff		SSCI Staff met with CGIP Staff
5 December 2001			Conference over FY 2002 Intel Authorization Act. Senate receded on CGIP entry.
28 December 2001	*Intelligence Authorization Act for Fiscal Year 2002* signed into law; the Coast Guard Intelligence Program entered the Intelligence Community.		

Figure 4. Timeline of CGIP Entry into the Intelligence Community
Source: Compiled by author.

Conceived in the uncertain times of the post-Cold War era, and involving a power struggle between Congress and the executive branch, the membership initiative was born in an era of transnational threats and concern for the government's agility in confronting these threats. Were the flexibility and multi-mission reputation of the Coast Guard, along with strong leadership within the Congress, the keys to overcoming resource-hoarding tendencies and bureaucratic inertia, and earning IC membership for America's smallest armed service? Or were the events of 9/11 the critical stimuli to CGIP IC entry? Why was CGIP entry a Congressional initiative? How does this case contribute to what is known about the management of intelligence within the U.S. system of government?

Passage without 11 September 2001

The opinions of interview subjects varied dramatically according to seniority. Most, but not all, of the senior policy advisors close to the legislation agreed[360] that this measure would have passed without the homeland security and antiterrorist focus created by the 9/11 attacks. Most of the mid-level staff felt that, without the influx of resources and a new mission focus, the CGIP-IC entry provision would have failed. Examination of this disparity illuminates the differing perception of power as it differs within the staff levels of the IC and various agencies.

---

360 A senior IC source, Chris Barton, Dennis Hager, and Commander Bernard. Admiral Papp believed the events of 9/11 were important to passage.

A senior Intelligence Community source who disagreed with Coast Guard IC inclusion, when asked whether the version would have passed without 9/11 replied, "Yes, I think it would have passed." The Chief of the Coast Guard Office of Intelligence from 1996 to 2001 and lead advocate for this initiative within the Coast Guard, Dennis Hager, was confident the measure would have passed without 9/11, stating in an interview "it was going to happen."[361] The Coast Guard Liaison Officer to the House of Representatives from 1998 until 2000, Commander Bernard, believed that the measure had built up enough momentum and that the events of 9/11 "made objecting to it that much harder."[362] Chris Barton, HPSCI General Counsel and the primary Congressional staff advocate, was equally confident that the Coast Guard Intelligence Program would formally join the IC, stating that the measure's sponsor, Representative Goss, was "a persistent man and the proposal stood on its merit."[363]

Six members of the CGIP staff believed that the measure adding Coast Guard intelligence to the IC would have failed without the tragic events of 9/11. These were the people who worked to refute the CMS arguments and endorsements opposing CG entry. They were concerned by stiff opposition from CMS, a senior-level advisory committee that represented the interests of even-more-senior IC officials. Admiral Papp shared concern, but for different reasons. He argued that "the terrorist events shaped everybody's thinking for a least a year....I'm confident that this would not have [otherwise] gained the traction it did at the time."[364]

Allegiance to hierarchical authority runs deep in the Coast Guard, and the phenomenon can easily explain the disparity in viewpoints. To a mid-grade officer, the Commandant of the Coast Guard is powerful, but to a member of Congress the Commandant, although an important person, cannot unduly influence that Congress member's decision. To the CGIP Staff, CMS was powerful. To the bureaucratically oriented CMS, the politically oriented intelligence committee chairman and Congress held the power.[365]

Based on the support of both Intelligence Committee Chairmen and numerous studies recommending greater access for border security agencies, the CGIP-

---

361 Hager interview.

362 Bernard interview.

363 Barton did not discount the effect the attacks had on this legislation, noting that "Post 9/11 the Coast Guard had proved itself particularly in NYC where they secured the port and directed the evacuation by sea of lower Manhattan. There was a recognition of the need and performance." Barton interview.

364 Papp interview.

365 The change in leadership of the SSCI may have been more pivotal than 11 September. Admiral Papp noted, "interestingly enough I believe that if the Republicans had stayed in power, Shelby would have been the [SSCI] Chairman. Because he was Chairman on Senate Select and Transportation Appropriations, he would have vetoed it [killed the provision in committee]. As it was, when power shifted to the Democrats, we had Barton and Goss (R-FL) supporting it on the House side and we had Democrats, Fillipone and Graham (D-FL), supporting it over the objections of the Republicans on the Senate side."

IC entry provision probably would have passed without the catalyst of the 9/11 attacks.

Why Congress?

The CGIP could have entered the IC through Presidential decree or joint designation by the DCI and Secretary of Transportation. Congress, however, acting through the HPSCI, felt a compelling need to ensure that the Coast Guard be specifically named in section 401(a) of 50 USC, the codified listing of the Intelligence Community. CGIP budget manager Ellen McCarthy offered an explanation for the Congressional initiative:

> The community didn't like this idea, but fortunately Congress understood the need. The timing was good as well. I think there were members of Congress who were frustrated by the failure to change focus in the IC. I think they saw our entry into the IC as a way to prod the IC into addressing issues like LE and Intel, sharing information, protecting the borders.[366]

Commander Lunday, the CGIP legal advisor, offered another theory: "There is so much resistance to amending Executive Order 12333 [in place since 1981], that legislative change is likely the primary avenue to membership. That is how the Department of Homeland Security, Information Analysis and Infrastructure Protection division, was added as the latest IC member."[367]

One motivation for Congressional action could have been to speed the reformation of the IC. Ellen McCarthy said, "I think that Congress absolutely had their eye on this as one way to prod the IC into changing." HPSCI Chairman Porter Goss, as a signatory on the Aspin-Brown Commission report advocating incremental change to address the post-Cold War threats facing the nation, already had deep familiarity with IC reform and organizational resistance to it. In a 26 September 2001 press release following unanimous HPSCI approval of the House version of the *Intelligence Authorization Act of 2002* (H. R. 2883), Goss said,

> [f]or the past six years, the Intelligence Committee has worked quietly but aggressively, and in a non-partisan manner, to address the intelligence issues that suddenly dominate today's headlines. Now, the audience is larger and the threats more immediate, but the Committee continues to press forward with sorely needed improvements....We remain united in our drive to work with the President and the Administration to build an Intelligence Community that has the capabilities that the U.S. will need to defeat terrorism and protect our national security. This is not a time to preserve the status quo, although there will be a tendency to do so as we embark on this war on terrorism. Now, more than ever, we must be bold

---

366 McCarthy interview.
367 Lunday e-mail.

in addressing our needs for intelligence—our first line of defense— and for our overall security.[368]

Given the "instinctive" bureaucratic resistance to change and the related instinct to protect budgets, Congressional legislation is the path of least resistance for adding members to the Intelligence Community. This case study documents both the bureaucratic efforts aimed at protecting resources, and the tendency to resist change to the IC. The case study of NIMA's creation by Anne Miles offers similar evidence. She points out that the creation of NIMA was carried out more easily inside Congress than if the bureaucracies of the IC and DOD had been more involved.[369]

In an opposing viewpoint the Coast Guard entry was a case of convergence of propitious timing. In this light, an emphasis on the homeland security mission, and threats that are ever more intractable, combined to make the Coast Guard an attractive addition to the Community. Even so, the inclusion of other new members by the same method would be unlikely. Even Chris Barton recognized that "this was a unique case. I don't think future agencies will enter the IC this way." Another argument against the conclusion that Congressional action is now to be the principal method of IC entry could be summed up as "once burned twice shy." Admiral Papp says of the IC,

> that having lost once, I suspect they would put up a more coordinated resistance. I think they underestimated the political support for the Coast Guard to do this on the Hill. And the fact that the key political supporters were the people in the best positions, both intelligence committee chairmen were on board with this. I don't think they would be likely to underestimate this happening again. I think they would take a little more action [than] they did.[370]

Another plausible explanation for Coast Guard entry as an atypical case is supported by the weakly worded objections in both DCI Tenet's letter and the draft CMS conference letter. It is clear that their objections were tepid. In the words of a senior IC source, "The Coast Guard issue was not worthy of a veto."

However, one must not forget that the process for the Coast Guard to enter the IC began two years before the terrorist attacks of 9/11. The language to include the Coast Guard was most likely entered into the bill during HPSCI conference and almost certainly before 11 September 2001. Barton and other advocates were lining up support on the Hill in the spring and summer of 2001.

---

368 Porter Goss, Representative (R-FL), statement after committee passage of H. R. 2883. Quoted in U.S. Congress, House, Permanent Select Committee on Intelligence, "House Intelligence Committee Approves Intelligence Authorization Act for Fiscal Year 2002," Press release, 107th Congress, First Session, 26 September 2001. URL:< http://intelligence.house.gov/hr2883.htm> , accessed 9 July 2001.
369 Miles, 22.
370 Papp interview.

With respect to a more unified resistance to change from the IC and DCI, the author's counter-argument is that the DCI allowed the measure to pass because the reasons for opposition—resources and mission relevancy—were "overcome by events." Once the decision had been made to include the Coast Guard Intelligence Program, the focus shifted from whether the Coast Guard should "have a seat at the table" to how to manage compliance with IC policies. Resolving this debate through Congress allowed for the DCI to refocus CMS and CGIP Staff on integrating Coast Guard assets into the IC.

Answer to the Research Question

"How may Coast Guard inclusion into the Intelligence Community through a HPSCI-sponsored initiative affect the future modification and management of the Intelligence Community?" This case represents the likely preferred, future method of modifying and expanding the Intelligence Community. The SSCI and HPSCI can come to agreement or consensus much faster than the disparate agencies of the Intelligence Community. Additionally, Congress's ability to legislate at the "strategic level" enables the reformer role sought by the HPSCI and SSCI. Congress approves only the concept. The details of enacting the legislation fall squarely on the shoulders of those subjected to the Congressional action. The process in this case boiled down to a measure that was two lines long, yet the Coast Guard Intelligence Program is still working toward compliance with Intelligence Community regulations and procedures.

Contribution to Congressional Oversight Literature

Congress will likely be the primary engine for the entry of new IC members, and the primary source of reform in the IC in succeeding years. This judgment is supported by the present study's corroboration of trends in Congressional oversight of the IC documented by Smist, Snider, and Miles. This publication provides an "inside" and detailed accounting of one Congressional initiative that has further shaped the IC, and an accounting that may have only been possible at this time, given the ephemeral nature of the electronic correspondence relied upon so heavily to document this case study. Smist and Snider provide macroscopic views of oversight in general. [371] As a case study, this publication complements the more detailed documentation of Congress's role in shaping the components of the IC started by Miles.[372] Although Congress may provide the "orthodox" future method of entry to the IC, it will not be able to impose its will in unopposed fashion. Presidential veto power will likely prevent any drastic or extremely contentious reform.

---

371 See Frank J. Smist, Jr., *Congress Oversees the United States Intelligence Community 1947-1994*, 2nd ed. (Knoxville,TN: The University of Tennessee Press, 1994); L. Britt Snider, *Sharing Secrets with Lawmakers: Congress as a User of Intelligence,* Monograph, Center for the Study of Intelligence (Langley, VA: Central Intelligence Agency, February 1997).

372 See Anne Daugherty Miles, *The Creation of NIMA: Congress's Role as Overseer*, Occasional Paper Number Nine (Washington DC: Joint Military Intelligence College, April 2002), for more information.

Conner's case study of the battle over the *Intelligence Authorization Act for Fiscal Year 1991* documents the only Presidential veto of an Intelligence Authorization Act.[373] This was the first-ever Intelligence Authorization Bill vetoed. President George H. Bush objected to the statutory definition of covert action, specifically its impact on foreign government and third parties, and vetoed the bill. In the wake of the Iran-Contra scandal, signing the bill would have changed the conception, execution and reporting of covert operations.[374] Congress may continue to lead IC reform, but the President of the U.S. always has veto power over any changes deemed excessive or encroaching on executive branch authority.[375]

Contributions of this publication

The documentation of the Coast Guard entry adds to the Congressional oversight literature. The successful exploitation of electronic media to capture and document the recent past may be the greatest contribution of this publication. This innovative method allows for the examination of evolving discussion and positions. The interagency and intra-office emails portray not only the positions but to a limited extent the personalities, politics, and working relationships involved in the series of decisions needed to formulate policy. In this case, the e-mail correspondence within the Coast Guard Offices of Intelligence and Congressional Affairs clearly expressed a tense relationship, due to the necessarily sensitive but direct liaisons between the HPSCI and CGIP Staffs. The CMS Staff and CGIP Staff interactions, as documented by interagency e-mails, grew increasingly contentious. CMS was initially indifferent toward funding the study but grew increasingly bothered until the CMS Staff finally excluded the CGIP Director from the BAH reports final briefing. The rawness of e-mail correspondence conveyed these unvarnished sentiments to the author before follow-up interviews were conducted. This method of exploiting the "instant history" captured in e-mails provides a new research tool that capitalizes on today's burgeoning technology to ascertain the persons, opinions, and strategies behind a decision. It also leads to questions about how this information may be preserved; ten years from now almost all of these e-mails will have been deleted and lost to researchers. Historically, researchers have enjoyed the luxury of waiting several years to assess the impact of time and change. The threat of our loss of these resources makes more immediate research almost necessary, and analysts no longer have the luxury of waiting to take advantage of the clarity of hindsight.

---

373 See William E. Conner, *Intelligence Oversight; The Controversy Behind the FY 1991 Intelligence Authorization Act, The Intelligence Profession Series Number Eleven* (McLean, VA: The Association of Former Intelligence Officers, 1993), 1.

374 Conner, 29-30, 35. Connor outlines the power struggle between Congress and the President; the subsequent FY 1991 bill, without the objectionable language, passed in August of 1991.

375 What would provoke a veto will remain unknown but Congress reduces the chance of veto by attaching changes to a "must pass" bill, typically appropriations bills.

Recommendations for Additional Research

BudgetaryImpact of IC Membership

How has IC membership affected the Coast Guard Intelligence Program's fiscal health? CGIP-IC membership opponents viewed the initiative as a resource grab, and some senior CGIP personnel did seek additional funding through joining the IC. Key questions associated with this question include: What is the trend of CGIP funding? How does the CGIP funding trend compare to those of other NFIP fund recipients? Was this change in funding a result of 11 September 2001 or of IC membership? A study of questions dealing with intelligence funding and budgets will need to be classified.

Workload Impact of IC Membership

Critics of CGIP-IC incorporation into the IC argued that the Coast Guard did not have the personnel to meet the obligations of being a named IC member. Richard Best, a national security specialist at the Congressional Research Service, stated in an interview that the personnel work-hours demanded by IC membership would be one of the biggest impacts on the Coast Guard. He suggested the Coast Guard Intelligence Program partner with the Office of Naval Intelligence (ONI) and follow a model similar to the Marine Corps, choosing carefully which meetings to attend and when to allow ONI to represent CGIP interests, in an effort to reduce the work-hours required. [376]

Commander Madsen, now assigned to the Coast Guard Intelligence Directorate, described the travails of the membership entry process:

> There is no model to follow for our entry into the IC; we are on our own. The CG is breaking new ground in this process and there is much spadework involved....The HPSCI's job is done; they asked the question and got us into the IC. Because no one else has joined the IC through a Congressionally directed action, most others [having] had their mission outlined as part of the *National Security Act of 1947,* the program faces an uphill battle.[377]

Commander Kevin Lunday, the CGIP staff attorney, described the impact IC membership had on his workload as substantial and challenging:

> The data calls and required reports for NFIP resources, the steps to achieve legal compliance (approved intel mission, approved 12333 procedures, define CG National Intel Element, train National Intel Element in 12333 procedures, build intel oversight/compliance structure, comply with

376 Richard Best, National Security Specialist, Congressional Research Service, interview by author, 23 April 2003.

377 Madsen interview.

pmyriad legal and DCID policy requirements for IC members) [are] almost endless.[378]

A thorough analysis of the work-hour costs of IC membership would be beneficial for future potential IC members. The research question might be, "What are the overhead costs of IC membership for the CGIP?" Key questions would include, "What are the one-time entry costs? What are the long-term work-hour costs? How many work-hours do IC membership meetings, reports, data calls, and budgets consume? What redundancies in workload occur as a result of IC membership?"

Inclusion of DHS into the Intelligence Community as a Case Study

An investigation could add to Congressional oversight case-study literature by examining the inclusion of the Department of Homeland Security into the IC as part of the *Homeland Security Act of 2002.* [379] The Intelligence component of this new department, the Information Analysis and Infrastructure Protection (IA/IP) division, was the next element to enter the IC after the Coast Guard. Examining the IC's reactions to the second element added in as many years could provide some insight into the concerns of the IC regarding expansion and management, as well as an assessment of the Community's ability to adjust to changing threats. Simultaneous investigation of the creation of the Terrorist Threat Integration Center by President Bush [380] and the DCI and its relation to the Department of Homeland Security would add to the body of knowledge regarding both the evolution of the IC and Congressional involvement in shaping it.

Checks and Balances, Leading and Following

This case study provides an example of how the U.S. system of government works to manage the Intelligence Community. In the early years of the IC, the executive branch exerted primary control, and initiated reform of the IC. To meet the challenges of the "space race" and emerging technology, the 1960s saw additional executive branch initiatives to consolidate and manage secret programs within the IC. In the Post-Cold War era this primacy has shifted to the Congress and resulted in numerous studies of the Intelligence Community, the creation of NIMA, and inclusion of the intelligence elements of the Coast Guard and Department of Homeland Security, all by Congressional actions.

---

378 Kevin Lunday, Commander USCG,staff attorney, Coast Guard Intelligence Directorate, e-mail to author, subject: "RE: CGIP entry into the IC," 20 June 2003.

379 *Homeland Security Act of 2002*, Public law 107-296 Sections 201 and 202, (2002).

380 White House, Office of the Press Secretary, "Fact Sheet: Strengthening Intelligence to Better Protect America," 14 February 2003, *Whitehouse.gov*, URL: <http://www.whitehouse.gov/ news/ releases/2003/02/print/20030214-1.html>, accessed 26 March 2003.

Chris Barton called the inclusion of the Coast Guard Intelligence Program in the IC "a systematic fix to a big problem. There are policymaker expectations in terms of maritime security functions, fulfillment of which required Coast Guard access, and its inclusion has already served the country well." He went on to explain the committee's vital role in incorporating the Coast Guard in the IC:

> [s]ometimes good ideas do not come from the executive branch. From time to time, the oversight functions of the intelligence committees give us a larger strategic view that informs our advocacy of new initiatives, such as the CGI [Coast Guard Intelligence] effort. At a staff level, we saw the intelligence gaps and the information sharing deficiencies that undermined the defense of our national maritime frontiers. Empowering CGI with the proper authorities and enhancing its budget and personnel roster addressed a significant and growing vulnerability in the U.S. homeland defense structure. This initiative was the right thing to do for the country. It really is that simple.[381]

Regardless of who initiates the change, the system of checks and balances allows each branch of the federal government an opportunity to initiate change. During the early evolution of the IC, the President led this campaign. Most recently Congress has taken the lead in IC reform.

---

381 Barton interview.

APPENDIX A

5 February 1999 Letter from Rep Porter Goss, HPSCI Chairman, to Admiral James Loy, Commandant USCG

TUE 15:57 FAX 202 225 1991

(202) 225-41

JOHN L MILLER, S
PATRICK B. MURI
MICHAEL W. SHE

U.S. HOUSE OF REPRESENTATIVES
PERMANENT SELECT COMMITTEE
ON INTELLIGENCE
WASHINGTON, DC 20515-6415

February 5, 1999

The Honorable James M. Loy
Commandant
U.S. Coast Guard
2100 Second Street, S.W.
Washington, D.C. 20593

Dear Commandant Loy:

Just a brief note to convey my appreciation to you for the assistance that Coast Guard personnel in Washington, Clearwater, and Port-au-Prince, Haiti provided to Chairman Gilman, Mr. Rangel, Mr. Conyers, and myself last week. With very short notice, Coast Guard did a first-rate job in providing essential support to CODEL Gilman in the Dominican Republic and Haiti.

Like you, I believe that the Coast Guard is a unique instrument for responding to emerging maritime security threats. As a member of the Aspin Commission, I argued fo a thorough reassessment of the Coast Guard's role within the United States national security structure and urged closer coordination between the Coast Guard and the intelligence community. As you develop the Integrated Deepwater System (IDS) to address Coast Guard's acquisition, personnel and operational requirements for the next quarter century, I hope that serious consideration will also be given to incorporating the Coast Guard as a full participant within the National Foreign Intelligence Program.

Once again, please accept my thanks for the Coast Guard's assistance. I look forward to meeting with you in the next few weeks on the evolving relationship of the Coast Guard with the intelligence community.

Sincerely,

Porter Goss
Chairman

APPENDIX B

28 November 2000 Letter from Mortimer Downey, Deputy Secretary of Transportation, to General Michael Hayden, Director of NSA

THE DEPUTY SECRETARY OF TRANSPORTATION
WASHINGTON, D.C. 20590

November 28, 2000

General Michael Hayden
Director, National Security Agency
9800 Savage Road
Fort George Meade, MD 20755-6000

Dear General Hayden:

I fully support the Coast Guard Intelligence Program Initiative. Part of this effort, as you know, is the establishment of a Service Cryptologic Element for the Coast Guard in partnership with the Naval Security Group and the Marine Corps. I believe this is an opportunity to improve intelligence support to Coast Guard missions, as well as improving foreign intelligence collection capabilities. I support this initiative and look forward to its approval and implementation. In this matter and in like matters regarding intelligence and national security issues, Rear Admiral James W. Underwood, Director, Office of Intelligence and Security, is my primary representative.

I look forward to increasing cooperation between the Coast Guard and the Intelligence community in a world that presents the broadest array of national security threats in our history.

Sincerely,

Mortimer L. Downey

APPENDIX C

DRAFT Letter from Norman Mineta, Secretary of Transportation, to Rep. Porter Goss, HPSCI Chairman (undated)

DRAFT

THE SECRETARY OF TRANSPORTATION
WASHINGTON, D.C. 20590

The Honorable Porter J. Goss
Chairman, House Permanent Select Committee on Intelligence
Washington, DC 20515

Dear Mr. Chairman:

I wish to express my strong support for your committee's intention to establish the U. S. Coast Guard as an element within the Intelligence Community under the National Security Act of 1947. I believe this action is especially warranted given the recent terrorist attacks perpetrated against our country.

The Coast Guard should be a member of the Intelligence Community. The Coast Guard brings unique capabilities - broad statutory authorities, extensive experience in asymmetric operations, unrestricted access to maritime industries - that are not duplicated elsewhere in the Intelligence Community. The Coast Guard is experienced in all intelligence disciplines, employs national assets to perform its missions and is a primary producer of intelligence products in areas such as maritime terrorism, counter drug and alien migration. There is no doubt that intelligence - derived from national sources as well as developed within our organization - is absolutely critical to the Coast Guard's ability to protect the nation's maritime transportation infrastructure, enforce its laws and treaties, operate as an Armed Service, and fulfill its obligations to Homeland Security. I strongly believe that operating as an element of the Intelligence Community is essential for the Coast Guard to exercise its responsibilities to meet the emerging threats to our nation's security.

I thank you for the opportunity to express my views on this matter.

Sincerely yours,

Norman Y. Mineta

DRAFT

APPENDIX D

4 December 2001 Coast Guard Intelligence Program "Bullets" for the Senate Select Committee on Intelligence Staff

04 December 2001

Coast Guard Membership in the Intelligence Community
Main Points

* The Coast Guard should join all of the other military services as a member of the Intelligence Community.

* The Coast Guard brings unique capabilities.

  - Broad statutory authority.
  - Extensive experience in asymmetric operations - leverage experience in drug law enforcement into other threat areas.
  - Unrestricted access to the maritime community all over the world (e.g. IMO and regional maritime organizations).
  - Access into geographic regions where the Navy and other government agencies cannot go (e.g. Cuba, Russian Border Guard).

* Congressionally chartered review of the Coast Guard Intelligence Program was completed and delivered to Congress in March 2001.

  - Rep Goss (R-FL) sponsored the FY2000 legislation that directed the study. Booz-Allen & Hamilton conducted the review.
  - Study highlighted: CG value as dual military service/law enforcement agency unique international access/worldwide maritime expertise.
  - Recommended membership in Intelligence Community.

* Community dissent to Coast Guard membership is based on incorrect perception that CG is attempting to get NFIP to pay for its intelligence program.

  - CG receives a very small portion of NFIP money (e.g., $11m/yr.)
  - In FY02 for every dollar of NFIP money received, the CG will be investing approximately $4.50 in their intelligence program.

APPENDIX D (CONTINUED)

4 December 2001 Coast Guard Intelligence Program "Bullets" for the Senate Select Committee on Intelligence Staff

04 December 2001

Coast Guard Membership in the Intelligence Community
Main Points (cont)

* It's important that Coast Guard gain membership in the Intelligence Community.

- Provides great access for community to CG and CG to the community.
- Progress at NSA to designate CG as a Service Cryptologic Element pends membership
- Validates CG existing contribution to the Intelligence Community.
- Satisfy collection/production requirements in LE, AMIO, homeland security.
- Legal authorities to maintain its collection program (e.g., broader SIGINT authority to conduct force protection and counter drug missions).
- CG brings unique maritime perspective to the IC
- Currently not at senior-level sessions, or only as second to Navy
- Without advocacy - some CG/maritime priorities never see daylight

BIBLIOGRAPHY

Allen, Deane J., and Brian G. Shellum eds. *Defense Intelligence Agency at the Creation 1961-1965.* Washington: DIA History Office, Defense Intelligence Agency, 2002.

Andrew, Christopher. *For the Presidents Eyes Only.* New York: Harper Colllins, 1995.

Arksey, Hilary, and Peter Knight. *Interviewing for Social Scientists.* Thousand Oaks, CA: Sage Publications, 1999.

Armed Forces/Subtitle A—General Military Law/Part I—Organization and General Military Powers/Chapter 1 – Definitions. 10 U.S.C. § 101.

Bamford, James. *The Puzzle Palace: Inside the National Security Agency, America's Most Secret Intelligence Organization.* New York: Penguin Books, 1983.

Babbie, Earl. *The Practice of Social Research,* 6th ed. Belmont, CA: Wadsworth Publishing, 1992.

Barton, Chris. Chief Counsel, House Permanent Select Committee on Intelligence. Interview by author, 16 June 2003.

Bernard, Al J., Commander, USCG (ret). Coast Guard Liaison Officer to the House of Representatives, 1998-2000. Interview by author, 22 April 2003.

_____. E-mail to Captain Jeffery Hathaway, USCG, and others. Subject: "Rep Goss/G-C meeting 2/25/99"(minutes). 26 February 1999. Obtained from Coast Guard Congressional Affairs staff , attached as Appendix A.

_____. E-mail to Captain Jeffery Hathaway, USCG, and others. Subject: "Expansion of CG role in Intl Community – MTG INTEL Subc.[sic], 15 March 1999.

_____. E-mail to Captain Jeffery Hathaway, USCG, and others. Subject: "Expansion of CG role in Intel Community – HPSCI"(minutes), 19 March 1999. Obtained from Coast Guard Congressional Affairs staff, attached as Appendix C.

Best, Richard. National Security Specialist, Congressional Research Service. Interview by author, 23 April 2003.

Best, Richard. "Coast Guard Intelligence." *Congressional Research Service Memorandum.* Washington, DC: Congressional Research Service, Library of Congress, 21 March 2002.

Best, Richard A. Jr., and Herbert Boerstling. "Proposals for Intelligence Reorganization, 1949-1996." A report prepared for the Permanent Select Committee on Intelligence, House of Representatives, *Congressional Research Service,* no number. Washington, DC: Congressional Research Service, Library of Congress, 28 February 1996.

Breckinridge, Scott D. *The CIA and the U.S. Intelligence System.* Boulder, CO: Westview Press, 1986.

Booz Allen & Hamilton. *Coast Guard Intelligence Program (CGIP) Study Program Management Plan.* McLean, VA: Booz Allen &Hamilton, 27 June 2000. Obtained from CG Congressional Liaison staff.

Boston, Rick, Lieutenant, USCG, Coast Guard District 14 Finance Officer. E-mail to author. Subject: "Operating Expenses for a 225' Buoy tender." 20 May 2003.

Buck, Alice L. *A History of the Atomic Energy Commission.* Washington, DC: U.S. Department of Energy, 1983. URL: <http://tis.eh.doe.gov/workstation/archives/fa118.pdf>. Accessed 23 May 2003.

Call, Fred R. (Joe) III, Commander, USCG (ret). Chief of Intelligence Operations, Resources and Planning, Coast Guard Intelligence Program (CGIP) 1998-2001, and assistant to Mr. Dennis Hager, Chief, CGIP. Interview by the author, 28 April 2003.

Central Intelligence Agency. "Conference letter on H.R. 2883." No date.

Clift, A. Denis. *Clift Notes: Intelligence & the Nation's Security*, 1st Edition. Washington, DC: Joint Military Intelligence College, 2000.

Coast Guard Authorization Act of 1998. Public Law 105-383. Section 308. (1998).

Commandant U.S. Coast Guard. Message to Coast Guard Commander Atlantic Area and others. Subject: "USCG Intelligence Program (CGIP) Study." 032200Z August 2000. Attached as Appendix D.

_____. Message to Coast Guard Commander Pacific Area and others. Subject: "Coast Guard Support to Navy Domestic Force Protection and Waterside Security Requirements." 182118Z January 2001. Attached as Appendix E.

Commission on the Roles and Missions of the United States Intelligence Community [Aspin-Brown Commission]. *Preparing for the 21st Century, an Appraisal of U.S. Intelligence.* Washington, DC: GPO, 1 March 1996. Available at URL: <http://www.access.gpo.gov/su_docs/dpos/epubs/ int/pdf/report.html>.

Conklin, Chris, Commander, USCG. Chief of Coast Guard District Fourteen, Operations and Law Enforcement Branch. E-mail to Arthur Hanson, Captain, USCG. Subject: "B-A Intel Study Brief." 24 August 2000.

Conner, William E. *Intelligence Oversight: The Controversy Behind the FY 1991 Intelligence Authorization Act*, The Intelligence Profession Series Number Eleven. McLean, VA: The Association of Former Intelligence Officers, 1993.

Cross, Terry, Rear Admiral, USCG. Assistant Commandant for Operations. Memorandum to Commandant USCG. Subject: "Congressionally Mandated Study of CG Intelligence Program," 11 December 2000.

Defense Intelligence Agency. "History-Intro." *DIA Homepage*, "History." URL:< http://www.dia.mil/History/40years/intro.html>. Accessed 23 May 2003.

Director of Central Intelligence. Director of Central Intelligence Directive 3/3, "Community Management Staff," 12 June 1995.

Downey, Mortimer L. Deputy Secretary of Transportation. Letter to General Michael Hayden, DIRNSA. No subject, 28 November 2000.

Drug Enforcement Administration. "DEA history section." *Drug Enforcement Administration Homepage*, "Concurrent Jurisdiction with the FBI (1982)." URL: <http://www.dea.gov/pubs/history/deahistory_03.htm#5>. Accessed 30 May 2003.

Elkins, Dan. *An Intelligence Resource Manager's Guide.* 6th printing. Washington, DC: Defense Intelligence Agency, 1997.

Ensign, Eric S., LCDR, USCG. *Intelligence in the Rum War at Sea, 1920-1933.* Washington, DC: Joint Military Intelligence College, 2001.

Establishment of the Coast Guard. 14 U.S.C. § 1.

"The Evolution of the U.S. Intelligence Community – An Historic Overview." Government Printing Office, n.d. URL: <http://www.access.gpo.gov/ intelligence/int/int022.html>. Accessed 23 April 2003.

Federal Bureau of Investigation. "Library and References Section." *Federal Bureau of Investigation Homepage* "History of the FBI; Origins 1908-1910." URL: <http://www.fbi.gov/libref/historic/history/origins.htm>. Accessed 27 May 2003.

_____. "History of the FBI: Early Days 1910-1921." URL: <http://www.fbi. gov/libref/historic/history/earlydays.htm>. Accessed 27 May 2003.

_____. "History of the FBI: Postwar America 1945-1960." URL: <http://www. fbi.gov/libref/historic/history/earlydays.htm>. Accessed 27 May 2003.

Federation of American Scientists Homepage. URL: < http://www.fas.org/irp/ offdocs/dcid3-3.htm>. Accessed 5 July 2003.

Fuss, Charles M., Jr. *Sea of Grass: The Maritime Drug War, 1970-1990.* Annapolis: Naval Institute Press, 1996.

Galemore, Gary. "The Presidential Veto and Congressional Procedure." *CRS Report for Congress* 98-156 GOV. Washington, DC: Congressional Research Service, Library of Congress. Updated 29 January 2001.

Gates, Robert. *From the Shadows. The Ultimate Insider's Story of Five Presidents and How They Won the Cold War.* New York: Simon and Schuster, 1996.

Goss, Rep. Porter (R-FL). Letter to Admiral James Loy, Commandant USCG. No subject, 5 February 1999.

Hager, Dennis. Chief of the Office of Coast Guard Intelligence, 1996-2001. Interviewed by author, 27 May 2003.

_____. E-mail to RADM Ernest Riutta, USCG, and others. Subject: "FW: Expansion of CG role in Intl Community – HPSCI." 22 March 1999.

_____. E-mail to Captain Robert Papp, USCG, Chief, Congressional and Governmental Affairs Staff, and others. Subject: "Intel Study Update." 9 February 2001.

_____. E-mail to RADM Terry Cross, USCG, and others. Subject: "FW: First Word On Coast Guard Study Brief To CMS." 27 February 2001.

_____. E-mail to LCDR Donald Jaccard, USCG, Congressional and Governmental Affairs Staff and others. Subject: "RE: Intel Study Review." 15 February 2001.

_____. Letter to Rear Admiral Terry Cross, USCG, Assistant Commandant for Operations. Subject: "Coast Guard Intelligence Program Study." 18 December 2000.

Hill, R. Cargill. "The NRO at Forty: Ensuring Global Information Supremacy." *NRO 40th Anniversary webpage.* n.d. URL:<http:www.nro.gov/40thann/NROHistory.pdf >. Accessed 23 May 2003.

Homeland Security Act of 2002. Public Law 107-296. Sections 201 and 202.

Holstein, James A., and Jaber F. Gubrium. *The Active Interview, Qualitative Research Methods*, Volume 37. Thousand Oaks, CA: Sage publications, 1995.

Intelligence Authorization Act for Fiscal Year 1993. Public Law 102-496.

Intelligence Authorization Act for Fiscal Year 2002. Public Law 107-108.

Intelligence Community Homepage. "Definition of the Intelligence Community." URL: <http: http://www.intelligence.gov/1-definition.shtml>. Accessed 11 July 2003.

_____. "Members of the IC: The Central Intelligence Agency." URL:<http://www.intelligence.gov/1-members_cia.shtml>. Accessed 23 May 2003.

_____. "Members of the IC: The Defense Intelligence Agency." URL: <http://www.intelligence.gov/1-members_dia.shtml>. Accessed 23 May 2003.

_____. "Members of the IC: Department of Energy: Office of Intelligence." URL: <http://www.intelligence.gov/1-members_energy.shtml>. Accessed 23 May 2003.

_____. "Members of the IC: Department of the Treasury: Office of Intelligence Support." URL: <http://www.intelligence.gov/1-members_treasury.shtml>. Accessed 23 May 2003.

_____. "Members of the IC: The National Imagery and Mapping Agency." URL: <http://www.intelligence.gov/1-members_nima.shtml>. Accessed 23 May 2003.

_____. "Members of the IC: U.S. Navy Intelligence." URL: <http://www.intelligence.gov/1-members_navy.shtml>. Accessed 23 May 2003.

Jaccard, Donald, Lieutenant Commander, USCG. Office of Congressional Affairs. E-mail to Ellen McCarthy, CGIP. Subject: "RE: Hill Staffer Briefings." 23 April 2001.

Johnson, Harvey, Rear Admiral, USCG. E-mail to Captain Robert Papp, USCG, Chief of the Office of Congressional Affairs, and others. Subject: "RE: Chairmen Goss letter and Intel Bill." 26 October 2001.

Joint Interagency Task Force East. "Fact Sheet." *Joint Interagency Task Force East Homepage.* URL:<http://www.jiatfe.southcom.mil/?cgFact>. Accessed 8 May 2003.

Joint Interagency Task Force on Coast Guard Roles and Missions. "Report of the Joint Interagency Task Force on Coast Guard Roles and Missions." URL:<http://www.uscg.mil/news/reportsandbudget/rolesandmissions/R&M.html >. Updated 10 February 2000. Accessed 16 May 2003.

Johnson, Loch. *A Season of Inquiry.* Lexington, KY: The University Press of Kentucky, 1985.

_____. *Secret Agencies U.S. Intelligence in a Hostile World.* New Haven, CT: Yale University Publishing, 1996.

Jones, Morgan D. *The Thinkers Toolkit, 14 Powerful Techniques for Problem Solving,* rev. ed. New York, Random House, 1998.

Kraninger, Kathleen. E-mail to Manson Brown and others. Subject: "Chairman Goss letter and Intel Bill." 25 October 2001.

Knott, Stephen F. "The Great Republican Transformation on Oversight." *International Journal of Intelligence and Counterintelligence* 13, no. 1 (Spring 2000): 49-63.

Larzelere, Alex. *Castro's Ploy—America's Dilemma: The 1980 Cuban Boatlift.* Washington: National Defense University Press, 1988.

Lowenthal, Mark. *U.S. Intelligence Evolution and Anatomy.* 2nd ed. Washington, DC and Westport, CT: The Center for Strategic and International Studies with Praeger, 1992.

Loy, James, Admiral, Commandant USCG. Memorandum to Secretary of Transportation, Norman Y. Mineta. Subject: "Coast Guard Wants to Join the National Foreign Intelligence Community," 29 March 2001.

McCarthy, Ellen. USCG Office of Intelligence, GDIP budget manager, 1998-2001. Interview by author, 26 June 2003.

Madsen, Reese, Commander USCG. Coast Guard Liaison Officer to NSA 1999-2002. Interviewed by author, 21 May 2003.

McCracken, Grant. *The Long Interview, Qualitative Research Methods*, Volume 13. Thousand Oaks, CA: Sage publications, 1988.

Michel, Chuck, Commander, USCG. Legislative Council, Office of Congressional and Governmental Affairs. Interview by author, 18 April 2003.

_____. E-mail to Captain Robert Papp, USCG Office of Congressional Affairs, and others. Subject: "RE: Chairman Goss letter and Intel Bill." 26 October 2001.

Miles, Anne Daugherty. *The Creation of NIMA: Congress's Role as Overseer, Occasional Paper Number Nine.* Washington DC: Joint Military Intelligence College, April 2002.

Mineta, Norman Y., Secretary of Transportation. Draft letter Rep. Porter Goss (R-FL), HPSCI Chairman. No subject. No date.

Morgan, Richard E. *Domestic Intelligence: Monitoring Dissent in America.* Austin, TX: University of Texas Press, 1980.

National Security Agency. *National Security Agency 1952-2002: Cryptologic Excellence: Yesterday, Today, Tomorrow* (50th anniversary monograph). Ft Meade, MD: National Security Agency, n.d. URL: <http://www.nsa.gov/images/50th_brochure.pdf>. Accessed 23 May 2003.

National Security Act of 1947. 50 U.S.C. § 401.

Office of Naval Intelligence. "Our History." *ONI homepage* URL: <http://www.nmic.navy.mil/history.htm>. Accessed 23 May 2003.

Olmsted, Kathryn S. *Challenging the Secret Government; The Post-Watergate Investigations of the CIA and FBI.* Chapel Hill, NC: University of North Carolina Press, 1996.

O'Rourke, Ronald. "Homeland Security: Coast Guard Operations-Background and Issues for Congress." *CRS Report for Congress* RS 21125. Washington, DC: Congressional Research Service, Library of Congress. Updated 8 October 2002.

Oseth, John M. *Regulating U.S. Intelligence Operations: A Study in Definition of the National Interest.* Lexington, KY: The University Press of Kentucky, 1985.

Ott, Marvin C. "Partisanship and the Decline of Intelligence Oversight." *International Journal of Intelligence and Counterintelligence* 16, no. 1 (Spring 2003): 69-94.

Papp, Robert, Rear Admiral, Chief, USCG Office of Congressional Affairs (1999-2002). Interview by author, 23 June 2003.

Papp, Robert Captain, USCG. Chief, USCG Office of Congressional Affairs. E-mail to Rear Admiral Harvey Johnson and others. Subject: "RE: Chairman Goss letter and Intel Bill," 26 October 2001.

Pershing, Ben. "Goss on a Mission." *Roll Call,* 4 October 2001. URL: < http://web.lexis-nexis.com>. Accessed 7 July 2001.

Poulin, Steve, CDR, USCG. CG Congressional and Governmental Affairs Staff. Email to Mark Sikorski, USCG. Subject: "RE: Intel Study One Page Brief," 23 February 2001.

Ranelagh, John. *The Agency: the Rise and Decline of the CIA,* revised ed. New York: NY: Simon and Schuster, 1987.

Relyea, Harold C. *Evolution and Organization of Intelligence Activities in the United States.* Laguna Hills, CA: Aegean Park Press, n.d.

Richelson, Jeffery, T. *The U.S. Intelligence Community.* Boulder, CO: Westview Press, 1999.

Riutta, Earnest "Ray," Rear Admiral, USCG. Chief of Operations. E-mail to Admiral James Loy, Commandant USCG. Subject: "Meeting with Chris Barton, House Permanent Subcommittee[sic] on Intelligence Staff," 13 January 1999. The HPSCI is a full committee.

_____. E-Mail to CDR Fred R. Call III, USCG, Dennis Hager, and others. Subject: "RE: Proposed Justification for CG Intelligence Program Study," 16 March 1999.

Schultz, Karl, Commander, USCG. Coast Guard Congressional Liaison Officer to the House of Representatives. E-mail to Dennis Hager, Chief, Office of Coast Guard Intelligence. Subject: "CG & MT Subcommittee Briefing on the CG Intel Program: Request for Weds 5/30 @ 1300." 21 May 2001.

Sikorski, Mark. Coast Guard Liaison Officer to the Booz Allen & Hamilton Study Group, Signal Corporation. Interview by author, 27 May 2003.

_____. E-mail to Dennis Hager, CGIP Chief, and others. Subject: "CGD7 Quick Look," 14 August 2001.

_____. E-mail to William Frentzel, BAH study project leader. Subject: "Box Score," 7 November 2000.

_____. E-mail to William Frentzel, BAH study project leader. Subject: "Re: CGIP Study Final Report Outline," 16 November 2000.

_____. E-mail to William Frentzel, BAH study project leader. Subject: "Re: Final Report Structure," 19 November 2000.

Smist, Frank J., Jr. *Congress Oversees the United States Intelligence Community 1947-1994.* 2nd ed. Knoxville,TN: The University of Tennessee Press, 1994.

Snider, L. Britt. *Sharing Secrets with Lawmakers: Congress as a User of Intelligence.* Monograph, Center for the Study of Intelligence. Langley, VA: Central Intelligence Agency, February 1997.

A source, senior Intelligence Community professional, who wishes to remain anonymous. Interview by author, 26 June 2003.

Sturtevant, Mary. "Congressional Oversight of Intelligence." *American Intelligence Journal* 13, no. 3 (Summer 1992), 17-20.

Stutz, Scott, Lieutenant Commander, USCG. CGIP Budgets and Planning Officer, 2001-2003. Interview by author, 30 April 2003.

Tenet, George J., Director of Central Intelligence. Letter to Rep. Porter Goss (R-FL), HPSCI Chairman. No subject. Date-stamped "HPSCI 11/07/01, 043107 PM."

Thomas legislative information on the Internet homepage. Library of Congress, 107th Congress Public Laws. "107-108" link. Bill Summary & Status section. URL: < http://thomas.loc.gov/bss/d107/d107laws.html>. Accessed 25 June 2003.

Thurber, James A., and Roger H. Davidson. *Remaking Congress: Change and Stability in the 1990s.* Washington, DC: Congressional Quarterly, 1995.

Townsend, Fran. Director, USCG Intelligence Program, 2001-2003. E-mail to Vice-Admiral Timothy Josiah, USCG Chief of Staff, and others. Subject: "FW: FY-03 Homeland Security Re-Rack," 7 November 2001.

_____. E-mail to Vice-Admiral Timothy Josiah, USCG Chief of Staff, and others. Subject: "Re: FW: LRM MGG169 — Central Intelligence Agency Conference Document onHR28," 29 November 2001

_____. E-mail to Vice-Admiral Timothy Josiah, USCG Chief of Staff, and others. Subject: "Update re: CIA," 12 November 2001.

_____. "The Man Who Knew." Interview by *PBS Frontline,* 30 May 2002. URL: <http://www.pbs.org/wgbh/pages/frontline/shows/knew/interviews/townsend.html>. Accessed 27 June 2003; McCarthy interview.

The Tower Commission Report. New York: Bantam Books and Random House, 1987.

Underwood, James, Rear Admiral, USCG. Director, Office of Intelligence and Security, Department of Transportation (DOT S-60). Memorandum to Secretary of Transportation, Norman Y. Mineta. Subject: "Coast Guard Inclusion in the National Foreign Intelligence Community," 28 March 2001.

U.S. Air Force Air Intelligence Agency. "History retrospective." *Air Intelligence Agency homepage.* URL: <http://aia.lackland.af.mil/homepages/ho/40s-2.cfm>. Accessed 23 May 2003.

U.S. Army Intelligence Center, Fort Huachuca. "A Brief History of US Army Intelligence." Fort Huachuca, AZ: Fort Huachuca Museums, n.d. URL: <http://usaic.hua.army.mil/History/PDFS/briefmi.pdf>. Accessed 23 May 2003.

United States Coast Guard. "Talking points for G-O (Assistant Commandant for Operations, Admiral Underwood). RE: Membership in the National Foreign Intelligence Community" 26 March 2001.

_____. "Talking points for G-O. RE: CMS Response to Coast Guard Intelligence Security/ MDA (Maritime Domain Awareness)," 27 March 2001.

_____. "Talking points for G-O. RE: Relationship of Intelligence Study to Homeland Defense/Security/MDA," 26 March 2001.

_____. "Talking points for G-C (Commandant) G-C Phonecon with Secretary Mineta," 28 March 2001. Obtained from Commander Michel, USCG.

_____. "S-1 talking points for Director OMB: On Coast Guard Intelligence Program Study," 29 March 2001.

_____. "Talking points for G-C (Commandant)/Rep Porter Goss (R-FL)," 25 February 1999.

United States Coast Guard, Office of Intelligence. "Coast Guard Membership in the Intelligence Community, Main Points." 4 December 2001. Attachment to e-mail from Ellen McCarthy, CGIP, to Captain Robert Papp, USCG Office of Congressional Affairs and others. Subject: "SSCI Request for Bullets – Time Sensitive." 4 December 2001.

_____. "US Coast Guard Intelligence Program Study." Internal memorandum. 4 August 2000.

_____. "Listing of Interview Candidates," n.d.

_____. Talking points,"G-C Meeting with Representative Goss (R-FL)." 15 March 2001.

US Coast Guard Deepwater homepage. URL: <http://www.uscg.mil/Deepwater/>. Accessed 20 June 2003.

US Coast Guard Rescue21 homepage. URL: < http://www.uscg.mil/RESCUE21/ home/index.htm>. Accessed 20 June 2003.

The United States Coast Guard: America's Lifesaver and Guardian of the Seas: A Guide to the U.S. Coast Guard. Tampa, FL: Faircourt LLC, 2002. URL: < http://www.faircount.com/ web04/coast/index.html>. Accessed 11 July 2003.

The United States Commission on National Security/21st Century [Hart-Rudman Commission]. "New World Coming: American Security and the 21st Century, Major Themes and Implications, the Phase I Report on the Emerging Global Security Environment for the First Quarter of the 21st Century." The National Security Study Group Homepage. "Reports." URL: <http://www.nssg.gov/ reports/NWC.pdf>. Accessed 23 June 2003.

_____. "Seeking a National Strategy: A Concert for Preserving Security and Promoting Freedom, the Phase II Report on a U.S. National Security Strategy for the 21st Century." The National Security Study Group Homepage. "Reports." URL: <http://www.nssg.gov/phaseII.pdf>. Accessed 23 June 2003.

_____. "Road Map for National Security: Imperative for Change, the Phase III Report on the U.S. Commission on National Security/21st Century." The National Security Study Group Homepage. "Reports." URL: <http://www. nssg.gov/phaseIII.pdf>. Accessed 23 June 2003.

U.S. Congress. House of Representatives. Committee On Rules. "108th House Rules," 108th Congress, 1st session, 2003. URL: <http://www.house.gov/rules/RX.htm>. Accessed 22 May 2003.

_____. House Select Committee to Investigate Covert Arms Transactions with Iran and Senate Select Committee on Secret Military Assistance to Iran and the Nicaraguan Opposition. *Report of the Congressional Committees Investigating the Iran-Contra Affair,* 100th Congress, 1st session, 1987. H. Rept. 100-433. S. Rept. 100-216.

_____. Permanent Select Committee on Intelligence. *Compilation of Intelligence Laws and Related Laws and Executive Orders of Interest to the National Intelligence Community.* 99th Congress, 1st session, 1985. Committee Print.

_____. "House Intelligence Committee Approves Intelligence Authorization Act for Fiscal Year 2002." Press release, 107th Congress, First Session, 26 September 2001. URL:< <http://intelligence.house.gov/hr2883.htm>. Accessed 9 July 2001.

_____. Permanent Select Committee on Intelligence. *Intelligence Authorization Act for Fiscal Year 2002,* 107th Congress, 1st session, 13 September 2001. H. Res. 2883.

_____. Permanent Select Committee on Intelligence. *Intelligence Authorization Act for Fiscal Year 2002, Conference Report.* 107th Congress, 1st session, 6 December 2001. H. Rept. 107-328.

_____. Permanent Select Committee on Intelligence. Report on *Intelligence Authorization Act for Fiscal Year 2002,* 107th Congress, 1st session, 26 September 2001. H.Rept. 107-219.

_____. Permanent Select Committee on Intelligence Staff Study. *IC21: Intelligence Community in the 21st Century.* 104th Congress (Washington, DC: GPO, 1996).

_____. Permanent Select Committee on Intelligence. *Intelligence Oversight Act of 1980.* 96th Congress, 2nd session, 1980. H. Rept. 96-1153.

_____. Select Committee on Intelligence. *Recommendations of the Final Report of the House Select Committee on Intelligence.* 94th Congress, 2nd session, 11 February 1976. H. Rept. 94-833.

_____. *Clerk of the House Homepage.* "Congressional History 106th Congress." URL: < http://clerk.house.gov/histHigh/Congressional_History/index.php>. Accessed 20 June 2003.

U.S. Congress. Senate. *A Resolution Establishing a Select Committee on Intelligence.* 94th Congress, 2nd session, 1976. S. Res. 400.

_____. *Intelligence Authorization Act for Fiscal Year 2002.* 107th Congress, 1st session, 14 September 2001. S. Res. 1428.

_____. Select Committee on Intelligence. *Confirmation Hearings of John Deutch.* 104th Congress, 1st session, 26 April 1995.

_____. Select Committee to Study Governmental Operations with Respect to Intelligence Activities. *Final Report of Select Committee to Study Governmental Operations with Respect to Intelligence Activities; Book I, Foreign and Military Intelligence.* 94th Congress, 2nd session, 26 April 1976. S. Rept 94-755.

U.S. Senate Homepage. Arts and History section. "Party Division." URL: <http://www.senate.gov/artandhistory/history/common/generic/party_division.htm>. Accessed 20 June 2003.

_____. "Senators who switch parties" link, URL: <http://www.senate.gov/artandhistory/history/common/briefing/senators_changed_parties.htm>, Accessed 2 July 2003.

U.S. Department of Transportation. *An Assessment of the U.S. Marine Transportation System, Report to Congress.* September 1999. URL: <http:www.dot.gov/mts/report/>. Accessed 23 June 2003.

U.S. Department of Transportation homepage. "U.S. Transportation Secretary Norman Y. Mineta." URL: < http://www.dot.gov/affairs/mineta.htm>. Accessed 23 June 2003.

U.S. President. Executive Order 11905. "United States Foreign Intelligence Activities." 18 February 1976.

_____. Executive Order 12036. "United States Foreign Intelligence Activities." 24 January 1978.

_____. Executive Order 12333. "United States Intelligence Activities." 4 December 1981.

_____. "The National Security Strategy of the United States of America." 27 September 2002.

_____. Office of the Press Secretary. "Fact Sheet: Strengthening Intelligence to Better Protect America." 14 February 2003. *Whitehouse.gov.* URL: <http://www.whitehouse.gov/news/releases/2003/02/print/20030214-1.html>. Accessed 26 March 2003

Van Wagenen, James S. "A Review of Congressional Oversight." *Studies in Intelligence* 1, no. 1 (1997):1-8. URL: <http://www.cia.gov/csi/studies/97unclass/wagenen.html>. Accessed 21 May 2003.

Warner, Michael. *Central Intelligence: Origin and Evolution.* Washington, DC: Center for the Study of Intelligence, CIA, 2001.

Yin, Robert K. *Case Study Research Design and Methods,* 2nd ed. Vol. 5 of *Applied Social Research Methods Series.* Thousand Oaks, CA: Sage Publications, 1994.

ABOUT THE AUTHOR

Lieutenant Commander Kevin E. Wirth is a native of Alden, New York. He graduated from the U.S. Coast Guard Academy in May 1992 with a Bachelor of Science in Marine Science. Upon graduation, he reported aboard the medium endurance Cutter USCGC CITRUS (WMEC 300) in Coos Bay, Oregon. After decommissioning the CITRUS in 1994 he served as a Maritime Law Enforcement Instructor at the International Training Division in Yorktown, Virginia. From the summer of 1997 to the summer of 1999, Lieutenant Commander Wirth was assigned to the Navy Afloat Training Group in Mayport, Florida where he conducted damage control, seamanship and navigation training onboard Coast Guard Cutters and Naval Warships. He served as the Executive Officer of USCGC LAUREL (WLB-290) from the summer of 1999 until her decommissioning in December 1999. Lieutenant Commander Wirth reported to USCGC WALNUT (WLB-205) in Honolulu, Hawaii where he served as the Executive Officer until the summer of 2002. Lieutenant Commander Wirth obtained a Master's Degree in Strategic Intelligence from the Joint Military College located in Washington, DC in 2003. Since that time, Lieutenant Commander Wirth has led the Current Intelligence Watch at Coast Guard Headquarters in Washington, DC, where his responsibilities included daily and crisis intelligence briefings to the Commandant and Senior Coast Guard leaders. In 2006 he was awarded the Department of Homeland Security Intelligence leadership award and took command of the 225-foot Coastal Buoy Tender ALDER (WLB-216) in Duluth, Minnesota.

www.ingramcontent.com/pod-product-compliance
Lightning Source LLC
Chambersburg PA
CBHW072059280526
45788CB00006B/2331